Sidelines

The Best of the Basketball Stories…

Mike Lunsford

Shade Tree Press

Shade Tree Press
8945 South Coxville Rd.
Rosedale, Indiana 47874
www.mikelunsford.com

Printed in the United States of America

The author and publisher gratefully acknowledge the *Terre Haute Tribune-Star* in which the contents of this book appeared in column form from October 1995 through January 2009.

Library of Congress Control Number: 2009906733

Lunsford, Michael J. (Mike), 1956-
Sidelines: The Best of the Basketball Stories…/
Mike Lunsford
ISBN 978-0-615-30731-2 (pbk.)

To the memory of my grandparents.

And to all who love the game.

-Contents-

3rd Quarter, Fall 2001-Winter 2003

4th Quarter, Fall 2004-Winter 2009

Overtime: Naming Names, and More...

Photographs

Additional Copies...

Copies of this book are available through the author's Web site at www.mikelunsford.com; shipping and handling charges will apply. School discounts are available. You can contact Mike Lunsford at hickory913@aol.com

-Introduction-
by Mark Bennett
Feature Writer for the Terre Haute Tribune-Star

Basketball purists marveled at Hoosier legend Larry Bird's court sense – his ability to somehow track the movements of the other nine players on the floor.

When it comes to telling stories about high school hoops in Indiana, Mike Lunsford possesses that same uncanny knack for seeing everything on the court, inside the gym and around the town. But Mike's talent transcends the news of Friday night's game. He knows the legends behind those framed pictures of tourney championship teams reverently hanging in the gymnasium lobby. He knows the radio play-by-play announcer perched behind the scorer's table. He knows the old coach, sitting quietly in the top row of the bleachers.

In that respect, Mike made me look like the Red Auerbach of Terre Haute journalism. The Boston Celtics president gambled and drafted Bird as a junior in 1978, knowing Bird wouldn't leave Indiana State University for another year. Auerbach figured Bird was worth the wait. Obviously, Red was right.

I was the sports editor of the Tribune-Star in 1995 when I asked Mike to write a regular column for us. The two of us had worked together as part-time sports writers at the newspaper years earlier, and I remembered Mike wrote with a distinct, folksy flair. We needed someone to give readers stories beyond the rebounds, winning streaks, and box scores. I figured Mike, who had become a high school English and history teacher, was the perfect choice. With some hesitance, he eventually said yes, while reminding me that his tenure probably would be brief, and warning me that he had no interest in critiquing the ups and downs of the Indiana Pacers. To me, those weren't disclaimers; they were virtues. I liked the idea of giving Mike an open door and an open slate. He could write anything he wanted and quit whenever he wanted.

That was 14 years ago. Mike never stopped writing his columns, and his growing legion of fans never stopped reading. I would love to claim that I knew Mike would become one of the most engaging writers ever to earn a byline in a Terre Haute newspaper. I'm not that clairvoyant. But, obviously, I made the right choice.

At the outset, Mike would submit his column and practically apologize for ruminating on bygone high schools' basketball team nicknames, or a tiny community's glory season from decades ago, or a coach's haircut policy. I was grateful that he veered off the beaten path; our readers were, too. Covering sports news is like an unending whitewater rafting trip, constantly documenting one dramatic turn or drop after another, analyzing what just happened, and preparing for the next big plunge. There's not much time to reflect deeply or exhale. As essential as that coverage is to fans of the sports pages, it's also refreshing to remember the smell of concession-stand popcorn, or the forlorn feeling of being the last guy on the team bench.

You'll enjoy Mike's literary sixth sense in this book, "Sidelines: The Best of the Basketball Stories..." High school basketball provides the perfect writing palette in Indiana. No game mattered more to the Hoosier culture in the 20th century. And while that connection has changed and evolved, its spirit remains in folks who came of age in the era when small-town Friday nights each fall and winter meant a trip to the gymnasium to watch the local boys play.

Rather than a breakdown of the elements of the game's box score, Mike's tales–over 60 of them, taken from his "Sidelines" columns written for the Tribune-Star from 1995 to 2009 – are more like a post-game gathering at the corner soda shop. Stories are told. While sharing a table, a burger and a milkshake with Mike, you might learn about high school teams such as the Cadiz Spaniards, Ireland Spuds, Alfordsville Yellow Jackets, Burns City Bees and the Sulphur Springs Blue Birds. You might hear about a courageous young coach at little Glenn High School in the 1950s, where he helped teach a small, mostly white community to accept and eventually embrace the black players on his talented team. You might rediscover the beauty of the season, too. Outside the gym, along the country roads leading to the school, Mike senses the signs of fall – the cool, crisp brink of Indiana's rekindled affair with basketball, when the glow of the sassafras reds and the tulip poplar yellows emerge. It's an annual moment of renewal and hope, still cherished in Indiana. As Mike puts it, "That's one thing I love about this time of year: while I'm busy remembering how good times used to be, I know the best things are yet to come."

That's true for you, the reader, too; the best stories, just a few pages away, are yet to come. Enjoy.

Warm-Ups...

Despite it being nearly 40 years ago now, I can clearly remember the day that my Grandpa Roy told me what I thought was an almost unimaginable lie. I was shooting baskets at my back yard goal—really no more than an old rim on a sheet of plywood tacked to a crooked locust pole—and since it sat near the east end of his huge garden, and he was hoeing strawberries, we stood and talked for a few minutes.

"You know, you won't be able to play that game forever," he said. "Someday soon you'll be grown up and you'll be working everyday."

He didn't say it to be cruel; he was a rough old bird who had quit school to help support his family long before even the tough times of the Great Depression came about. He'd mined coal and dug ditches and dipped enameled pots and pans in his hard-scrabble lifetime, and despite the fact that we rarely missed a winter Saturday afternoon together watching a Purdue game on the television, he really didn't see the value in playing basketball when a young man could be earning a dollar with his hands and back and sweat.

"I think you're wrong," I told him as I stood there in high tops and cut-off blue jeans and in need of a haircut. "There won't be a day that goes by from now on that I won't have one of these in my hands," I said as I rolled a worn Voit basketball in my hands. "I'm going to play basketball until I'm your age," I added.

He didn't argue; he just went back to his work and listened to the endless pounding of that ball on the packed sandy dirt of my private arena...I went on from those days long ago to a rather inglorious career as a player, a slightly better career as a coach, and I'm still working at one as a writer. I started the latter vocation writing about sports, most of all about basketball, and after my years as both player and coach were gone, I still write, at least a little, about the sport I was certain I would play forever.

Just a few years after I left coaching—voluntarily, I might add—I got a call from a friend who just happened to be the sports editor of the Terre Haute Tribune-Star. If you're reading this book from cover to cover then you know already that it was Mark Bennett, and that he asked me to start writing a basketball column; "Sidelines" was born. In those first few years, I didn't write but a handful of stories, but by the third season Mark had a hard time getting me to shut up.

This book is a compilation of what I hope are the best stories I have written about what Hickory Huskers' guard Wilbur "Shooter" Flatch called "the greatest game ever invented." At least, these are some of my favorite stories.

Hopefully, most of the columns in this book have stood the test of time; some, perhaps, have not. I believe that it has taken a long while to get my writing legs under me. I'd like to believe that I've learned a little about my craft since I started writing for the newspaper years ago, but I'll have to let you be the judge of that.

Before I wind this up, I had better thank a few people who helped make this book a reality. I want to thank my buddy, Mike Hardesty. Simply put, Mike knows computers; when I have a technical problem, Mike solves it. Bill Wolfe, a talented artist and sculptor comes next; Bill graciously did the art work—the old backyard basketball goal—that you see from time to time in this book. I envy Bill's talent, but I value his friendship more.

This book would not have happened had it not been for the good folks at the Terre Haute Tribune-Star. Besides Mark, fellow sportswriters Andy Amey, David Hughes, Tom Reck, and Todd Golden, among so many others who have gone on to other newspapers and careers, helped me get my stories into print. I also want to thank Jimmy Claus and Carl Bender; Jimmy was editor of the old Tribune years ago, and it was he who first sat me down at a typewriter and told me that as soon as I discovered where the letters were, I could be a writer. Carl was perhaps the toughest teacher I ever had, and I thank him for it now, although I certainly didn't do it then. Thanks also to Max Jones, the paper's managing editor, and Susan Duncan, too; I write it, and they print it.

As usual, I have to thank my wife, Joanie. She's been my sounding board, extra editor, and voice of encouragement for this book and will continue to be for the books to come.

Finally, thanks to my readers. Like any good coach, you've rewarded my hard work by giving me a chance to play.

My granddad was right, of course. Most of my days now go by without my even looking at a basketball; I quit playing pick-up ball in the local high school gym after I turned 50, that coming after I hobbled on a sore knee at work for three weeks.

I wasn't able to play the game forever, but I still shoot a little on the goal I put up for my son in our backyard.

I can still dream, can't I?

Mike Lunsford, 2009

"It's not so important who starts the game but who finishes it."

John Wooden

"Take care of all your memories, for you cannot relive them."

Bob Dylan

"Be true to your work, your faith, and your friends."

Henry David Thoreau

The Best of the Basketball Stories…

First Quarter
Fall 1995-Winter 1999

The Best of the Basketball Stories…

******Author's Note: The following column was included in this book, not because it was my best story, but because it was my first.***

With a nostalgic flavor, thoughts flowing again
October 25, 1995

This is not my first attempt at column writing. Twenty years ago, I was the sole sportswriter, sports editor, and columnist in a neat little country weekly, the now-defunct Fontanet Gazette. The paper cost a whopping 15 cents a copy — $5 a year for a subscription.

I typed about a thousand words a week on my portable Smith-Corona typewriter, drove the column over to the printer myself, and scrounged around for any black and white photo I could find that was remotely related to sports.

The column, called "From the Sports Corner," was an eclectic collection of high school basketball, professional football, and editorial commentary. At least I can say that the newspaper died before I received many negative reviews.

It would be nice to think that every sportswriter who writes a column in the local newspaper knows what he or she is writing about. I didn't know much 20 years ago, have improved on the situation very little; I'm probably not going to fool you now. I'm getting to an age when talking about sports is much easier than participating in them. In other words, "shooting around" has officially replaced "working out."

This column is to appear "occasionally" in the Tribune-Star. I use that term because I don't intend to give up my day job(s) in order to do it.

This winter I intend to write about things and people I care about. I don't believe for a second that readers will pick up a copy of this newspaper to read my views about recent trades or upcoming professional games. I intend to keep a leisurely pace, a porch-swing attitude, a courthouse bench point of view.

That old typewriter of mine sits idle in a seldom-opened case near my desk now, and since the height of its glory, quite a bit has changed. In my opinion, there are some issues and people who can stand some ink, and I plan to spend a little time discussing them. As a coach for years, and as a writer for a few more, I've met quite a few interesting people who embody what I think athletics are about. But sports have evolved since Jimmy Claus first hired me out of a sophomore journalism class at Indiana State to write on the weekends for the old Terre Haute Tribune.

Whether I like it or not, class sports are here to stay, at least for a while. Many fans believe that classes might rejuvenate high school basketball. For the game's sake, I hope they're right. I suspect that there are other reasons why we can't seem to regain the small-town, big-spirited feeling that leaked at the seams of any gym you walked into on any Friday night not so many years ago.

I still think that the spirit of athletics lives best in children that have had less coaching and larger backyards in which to play. I think that the tears so often displayed at press conference post-mortems, like those for the fired Bill Mallory, are more often than not, authentic. I think that we're taking some of the fun out of sports.

There you have it. I'll be nostalgic and maudlin and opinionated, and I'll rarely pull fodder for my columns off ESPN or the wire services. I don't even have cable television yet; I enjoy good books instead. I'm not on the Internet, and I don't accept email; I still like getting hand-written letters.

Mind you, I'm all for technology — I don't exactly write my stories on cave walls with charcoal — but for everything that computers and satellites have given us, they've taken from us as well. The human element, including weakness and failure, is still the most interesting thing sports have to offer us.

I like to sit down and talk with people, when I have the time. People like Bernard Gideon, who coached, and chose to stay, in a small town like Montezuma forever; people like Mike Hoevet, who runs The Wellness Center in Clinton, but who will talk sports — any sports — to anyone at any time; people like Jim Chaney, who can still hit the two-handed set-shot like he did back in the 50's for Rosedale High School; and people like Megan McFarland, who at age 9, still thinks her basketball team did "pretty good," despite being held scoreless in its weekly Saturday afternoon game a few weeks ago.

To be honest, I've had my fill of expert analysis and color commentary. Sports and sports columns should be about people.

Readers of this column had better get used to a steady diet of Bernards and Mikes, Jims and Megans, because that's who I know. I think they're what watching sports is all about.

'Coach' cherishes memories, but also likes changes
November 16, 1995

Bernard Gideon has been known as many things: teacher, gentleman, father. But to most who know him, or those who wish most to thank him, he'll always be "Coach."

Born in the tiny southern Indiana burg of Algiers in 1927, Gideon went on to graduate from Oakland City College and began a high school coaching career that spanned nearly 35 years, most of them at tiny Montezuma High School in Parke County. By the numbers of young coaches who regularly make their way to him for advice, it could be said that he still coaches.

"I graduated from Oakland City in 1951 with a degree in physical education and social studies and got my first job at a little school called Bogard Township, down in Daviess County," Gideon said. "I stayed there four years and then moved over to Elmore Township. After two years there, I came up here (Montezuma)."

Gideon played basketball and baseball at Petersburg High School, worked two years after graduation, and was offered an athletic scholarship to Oakland City College after the coach there saw him play for the "Petersburg Independents," a local basketball team.

While just a freshman in high school, and later in college, Gideon came to know Gil Hodges, who went on to a stellar professional baseball career and eventually managed the "Miracle Mets" to the world championship in 1969. Gideon and Hodges played both baseball and basketball.

"[Hodges] was a good boy. In fact, I drove to school with him. After he went away to play at St.

Joseph's, near Rensselear, he came down to play at Oakland City. He didn't score a whole lot, but he sure could do the rest of it. He had hands that were three times bigger than mine."

About his first coaching jobs Gideon said, "Oh, we only won five or six games a year down there, but that was pretty good really. We didn't play very many in the first place, and we only had about 60 kids in the school." He came to Montezuma in the fall of 1957 and coached for thirty years.

Gideon has seen changes in about every phase of coaching and playing high school and college basketball. He likes quite a bit of what he sees. "If you look at the 40's to now, overall, ballhandling has improved. Kids do things now that they didn't or couldn't do then — and they're bigger. If I had a kid who was a six-footer, well, I had a big guy. Now, kids being 6'5" or 6'6" isn't unusual at all."

Gideon added, "The game is more freely played now. We used to have a lot of set stuff. Pressure defenses won't allow that as much these days."

He also sees class basketball as a sign of the times. Montezuma was the largest school at which Gideon ever coached—about 160 students— and he still ended up playing at Terre Haute North in the sectional tourney as his career came to an end.

"I think [class] has a lot of merit to it. If you're a coach that works hard and then has to face those big schools in tournament… Well, you'd know what I mean. [The big schools] have the horses. I think, other than more travel, it will be a good thing for small schools."

Gideon recalls when Parke County had at least nine

high schools, all of them the focal points of their communities, "There were schools in Mecca and Bloomingdale and Bridgeton and Tangier. Basketball was real interesting; you played some [county schools] home and home, so there was a rivalry.

"When I coached, our biggest games were against Rockville and Rosedale. The neighborhood schools were hurt by consolidation. Those little towns that were just eight or ten miles apart really battled. Now it's seventy or eighty miles, and those rivalries don't mean as much."

"Old Sharpie [Howard Sharpe] had the three Andrews boys down at Terre Haute. We didn't have that kind of talent up here. That's one place where class has to help. We played all of the big Terre Haute clubs."

"We played in some small gyms, and then when we played in big places, it really gave our kids trouble. I remember one gym down in Winslow and another over in Scotland, Ill. They had stoves in the corners near the court. You had to keep the players from getting burned. But those little gyms helped the game."

Gideon also commented on his own coaching style: "Sportsmanship was expected. I was pretty strict. I wasn't past getting on the phone to make sure the boys were home, and if one wasn't home, I'd have to bench him. Sometimes you hurt yourself. The kid you sit down might be your star."

Gideon's calm demeanor belies his competitiveness. One of his assistants recalled hearing him humming while he sat on the bench during games. "In these days, you're running all the time, but when I coached, I often had to say 'Settle down, set it up, and work for a good shot," Gideon said.

Despite some recent health problems, Gideon still watches quite a bit of basketball, from grade school to college, but he doesn't watch the pros. "I'm going to watch Montezuma's fifth and sixth grades play tonight, and I'll enjoy that as much as anything. I watch very little of the pros. It's too rough and undisciplined. I'd rather watch a junior high game than the Pacers any day."

One of the major changes Gideon has seen is in girl's basketball. "It's [girls ball] much improved. I remember when girls just threw it at the basket. There's some awfully good shooters out there now. Girls know the game better, and they shoot the ball much better. I've enjoyed watching them."

Gideon didn't want to offend anyone by mentioning his best team or best players, but some of the top high school players he ever saw played for the Washington Hatchets when they won the back-to-back state championships in the early 40s. "They had a player named Charlie Harmon — a terrific jumper. Now that had to be a great team to win the state twice. They had a guard named Art Grove too. He was the first I saw that put the ball behind his back."

"I had some real good kids too. Wiley Budden was one of the better ones; Denny Hesler, around 1958 and 59, was another. Terry Gill was terrific for us in the late 60's. There's so many. I'd say that the one thing they had in common though, what real good players have in common, is they could handle the ball. With the pressure players face today, they had better work on their ball handling."

Coaching has meant everything to this venerable observer of the game. "Through coaching I've met a lot of nice fellows; that's by far the best thing,' Gideon said.

"I don't know what would have happened to me had I not had that scholarship to college. We didn't have much when I was a boy. Sports defined what I made out of my life. I made a living, but I also met so many good people."

He added, "My best memories are of the kids—watching them get better. I guess the biggest thing is seeing kids develop as players, as students, as people. I had some pretty good kids."

They had a pretty good coach too.

Backyard hoops a place to live dreams, learn lessons
November 20, 1996

In the opening scenes of "Hoosiers," Hickory High's new coach, Norman Dale, wheels his old Chevrolet coupe past barnyards and playgrounds where kids are playing basketball in T-shirts, blue jeans, and black canvas high-tops.

Although I wasn't even thought of in the early 50's, I can still connect with that film. My cousin was a star at a little country school when I was a kid, and I know that high school basketball was almost a religious experience in those days as we headed off at dusk in my uncle's car for games at Staunton and Bainbridge. No matter how many times I've been to Assembly Hall, Mackey Arena, and Market Square Arena, I remember more about the muddy spots of ground on which I played with my friends.

The shoes may have been white by then, but they were still Chuck Taylor All-Stars or Red Ball Jets, and the hours seemed to fly by until the darkness, or the cold, or our moms put an end to the day for us.

When I was in eighth grade, my dad put up my first basketball goal after I'd pestered him for months. My arena consisted of an old locust pole, a three-quarter inch sheet of plywood — which I painted generously as part of the deal — and a well-worn and slightly crooked rim that my cousin had donated.

The rim was too old to have the brackets from which the net hung, so it required at least a half a roll of black electrician's tape to keep the net firmly in place. The rain turned my court to muck, and I vividly remember scraping the snow off the ground to play in the winter. I had two basketballs for good reason: one was kept on the heat register while I played with the other until it was too cold to bounce.

In other words, I was no different than thousands of other young fanatics who lived, breathed, and ate basketball. I was one of many who played in old brown cotton gloves and a stocking cap; one who played in the rain working against imaginary defenders in imaginary games. We were all Jimmy Chitwoods with winning shots at buzzers we heard only in our heads every day after school.

We played in Dave Price's barn lot, watching where we stepped; in Donnie Gambill's backyard; under Doug Hawkins' hay mount, careful to avoid spilled soybeans on the concrete; at Jim Huxford's, Jim Chaney's; and behind Kenny Mattick's parents' garage with its huge 8-foot backboard.

In those private games, I most often became "The Rocket," also known as Rick Mount, the Purdue All-American. It was a great thrill years later to meet Mount when I bought practice clothes and basketballs for my own high school team from his sporting goods store. Needless to say, not one of my players had ever heard of Rick Mount, and they were baffled by how reverently I spoke of him.

I'm not alone in fondly remembering those days "shooting hoops." Ross Didier and Dave Gilstrap were typical players brought up on backyard basketball. "I wouldn't trade the time I spent with my friends in the backyard for anything," says Didier, 40. "I remember how rough it was, but I worked on shots that I couldn't practice at school."

The 1975 West Vigo grad also recalled some friends who played with him. "Mostly we'd play at the Seventh Street courts or over at the elementary school," said Didier. "We'd go down to the goals at the school—they were only about nine feet—and we'd dream we could jump. We didn't get there that much, but Charlie Vicars even had a full-court in his backyard. We had the grass worn down to the dirt all the way around it."

"Sure, we'd get into fights. You couldn't play with the Cates brothers [Bud and Lee] without that, but it taught me a lot. I'd watch a game on television and then go out and try to work on the moves I'd seen. It was so competitive, and I was a better player for it. They [the Cateses] were the most competitive people I've ever seen."

"When a coach was around you'd feel restricted," Didier added. "But when you got out with your friends, you could be as creative as you wanted to be. That helped me a lot. I was never a real physical player before, but you had to be when you played with those guys, or they'd eat you up."

Gilstrap, a 1963 graduate of Salem High School, just north of New Albany, remembers, "We had a goal at home, and I was fortunate that there was an old grade school next door to where we lived. I played there all the time. I wanted to work at it and get better. That was what summers were for."

"We never had the chance to get inside, so in the summer that's where we did all of our playing. There were no summer leagues and the like then. We were on our own. We had to work at it, you know. You had to motivate yourself then. I think everything today is geared for playing in a gym."

"Another difference I see too is that we kept our equipment in good shape," says the teacher and deputy sheriff. "We took care of it because that's all we had. A lot of kids now can't get someplace good to play because everything is torn up before they can use it. They have a hard time finding a safe place to play."

Backyard basketball may be a dying variation of the sport. The friendship and basketball that mingled on those courts were totally unsupervised: no parents, no coaches, no referees.

We learned, most often peacefully, to handle our disagreements, and if we couldn't, somebody just took his ball and went home.

A whole new language developed too. You "checked it" when you played at only one basket; you could play "make it, take it" if it was a grudge match; you "spotted" somebody if you were in a betting mood; you almost always played "shirts and skins."

Today's leagues and camps and programs are doing admirable work. They give kids places to play and compete. Young players now are undoubtedly getting better instruction at earlier ages than ever before. But, in an age when those things were simply not around, kids spent time alone, or in the company of their friends, learning to play a game that they still love and imagining that they could be the best.

Consolidation sees end of dozens of local schools
November 26, 1997

The Wabash Valley has a rich high school basketball tradition, much of it steeped in an era when every little town and village had a school to call its own. I've written about a good number of those schools of years past, whose glory days dried up when consolidation came knocking on their doors.

I've also discovered first-hand that there is considerable interest out there in the old days. A friend of mine recently showed me an Indianapolis Star on-line forum that was entertaining readers to discuss favorite school nicknames.

Three that were mentioned were the Owensburg Boogers, the Summitville Goblins, and the Smithville Skibos. A quick glance at a state map suggests that there is only one Owensburg in Indiana. That was in Greene County, and they were called the Indians.

I could handle being a proud Polecat from Poling or a Yeoman from Upland. I wouldn't mind even being a Skibo—if I knew what one was—but I would have to draw the line at being a Booger.

The combination of small schools was often a necessity, but it was rarely done without controversy. Lost along with the schools were some of the fiercest rivalries and most endearing images of school life. Records are nowhere near complete, but I am amazed by the number of schools that once thrived in our area through the years. Some outlived belted silk trunks and double mid-court lines, but many were gone well before World War II.

At one time, Vigo County was the home of the Fontanet Beantowners, the Glenn Pirates, the Blackhawk Chieftains, the Honey Creek Honey Bees, the Otter Creek Otters, the Pimento Peppers, the Prairie Creek Gophers, the Riley Cossacks, the Garfield Purple Eagles, Gerstmeyer's Black Cats, State High's Young Sycamores, Schulte's Golden Bears, Concannon's Cannons, the West Terre Haute Bobcats, Wiley's Red Streaks, and the New Goshen Falcons.

IHSAA membership records also show that several more short-lived high schools also existed in Vigo County, and that consolidation wasn't just a phenomenon of the 1950s and 60s either.

For instance, Prairieton consolidated with Honey Creek in 1927. Terre Haute Rankin combined with Otter Creek, and Terre Haute Thornton was swallowed by Glenn, both schools gone by the mid '30s. Clay County may be down to two high schools now, but at one time basketball fans could have traveled to Ashboro to watch the Shamrocks, driven to Bowling Green to see the Pioneers, watched the Cardinals in Coalmont, the Apple Boys in Cory, the Yellow Jackets at Staunton, Van Buren Township's Blue Devils, Brazil's Red Devils, or the Clay City Eels.

Vermillion County, also a two high school county now, at one time touted the Cayuga Indians, Clinton's Wildcats, the Dana Aggies, the Hillsdale Hilltoppers, the

Newport Tigers, the Perrysville Eagles, and the St. Bernice Hornets, while Fountain County schools included the Hillsboro Wildcats, the Mellott Derbies, Newtown (apparently had no nickname), the Veedersburg Green Devils, the Wallace Peppers, and the Kingman Black Aces.

Parke County, bucking the trend with three small school corporations still going, boasted at least 11 schools at one time. Among those were the Bellmore Golden Eagles, the Bridgeton Raccoons, the Greene Township Aces, the Marshall Bobcats, the Mecca Arabs, Montezuma's Aztecs, the Rosedale Hotshots, the Tangier Tigers, the Rockville Rox, the Bloomingdale Bulldogs, and Bloomingdale Academy's Immortals.

Putnam County has a long hoops heritage too. One of the top programs was that of the Bainbridge Pointers, who squared off regularly with county foes such as Belle Union's Panthers, Clinton Center's (Was that near Clinton Falls?) Yellow Jackets, Fillmore's Cardinals, Putnamville's Bulldogs, Reelsville's Indians, the Roachdale Hawks, the Russellville Bees, the Greencastle Tiger Cubs, and the Cloverdale Clovers.

Sullivan County schools included the Carlisle Indians, the Dugger Bulldogs, the Fairbanks Trojans, the Farmersburg Plowboys, the Graysville Greyhounds, the Hymera Shakamaks, the Merom Beavers, the New Lebanon Tigers, the Pleasantville Blue Streaks, the Shelburn Panthers, and the Sullivan Golden Arrows.

On Friday nights through the winter, Greene County fans spent their evenings watching the Jasonville Yellow Jackets, the Lyons Lions, the Midland Middies, the Owensburg Indians, the Scotland Scotties, the Solsberry Hornets, the Linton Miners, the Marco Bears, the Bloomfield Cardinals, and the Worthington Ramblers. Newberry apparently carried the moniker of the River Rats.

Owen County was home to the Freedom Aces, the Coal City Colts, the Gosport Indians, the Patricksburg Bulldogs, the Quincy Aces, and the Spencer Cops, all top rivals.

It may very well be true that consolidation paved a way for better educational opportunities, and no one is in a hurry to turn back the clock. But as is the case in all good schooling, there was a very high price to pay.

Nothing can keep this Purdue fan far from the court
November 26, 1997

Stacey Greene sees the world from a height of 4 feet or so, yet she dreams about life above the rim. A "nearly 16-year-old" sophomore at Riverton Parke High School, she has never let her wheelchair or walker keep her off a basketball floor.

Facing a life challenged by spina bifada, a condition at birth that exposes the spine, Stacey keeps a smile on her face, belying the trouble she tackles daily from her knees to her feet.

"I've always thought about playing basketball," Stacey says, "Twenty-four and seven, but I haven't found a place to play."

Until last year, she attended a summer basketball camp, working on her free throw shooting, and being with other players her age. She already knows she wants to go to college and become a computer analyst. In the meantime, she's found a capable substitute for playing—

the Purdue Boilermakers, and their coach, Gene Keady.

Being a huge Purdue fan in a household with two rabid Indiana Hoosiers supporters—sister Melissa is a freshman at IU—Stacey is not faint of heart and without an opinion. Her devotion to Purdue was rewarded when she met Keady in 1996.

"We met at a game [in West Lafayette]. My dad wrote Coach a letter and set it up with him after the game. I was hoping that Purdue would win because I knew he [Keady] would be in a better mood. They won," Stacey said.

"I was stunned to meet him. It was cool because I also got to meet a few players. I met Chad Austin, Todd Foster, Brandon Brantley, and some others."

Why not support IU when her dad, Cliff, and Melissa live and die by what goes on in Bloomington? "I don't like Bobby Knight. I don't like his actions. I went to a Purdue-IU football game at IU, and I wore my Purdue sweatshirt, and I wasn't the only one. I just like the way Coach Keady teaches defense. I always watch The Gene Keady Show," Stacey explained.

Stacey says she is a little upset that Melissa will be at the IU-PU match-up at Bloomington this winter, while Stacey's seat will be in front of the family television.

"I'm so mad. She [Melissa] loves Luke Jimenez. I kind of like him too, but I'm sending my camera down to her, and I want her to take Purdue pictures with it."

Who are Stacey's role models? Obviously, people who are involved with Purdue basketball. "Well, Coach Keady for one. I know he has a scowl on his face much of the time, but once you see him in person, you'd see he's not like that. He's actually a very nice man," Stacey said.

"I also like Stephanie White because she can do it all. But I also like her because she seems like a good person; she seems down-to-earth."

Nearby much of the time is Stacey's mother, Sherri, who is often chauffeur, therapist, and best friend. The devotion she and Cliff show their daughter helped create a wonderfully independent young lady.

"At least she's not a big IU fan," Stacey says of her mother. "She's let me have my room all-Purdue!" Besides basketball and baseball (she cheers the Orioles, Braves, and Mariners), Stacey loves to swim. "They call me a fish," she says of her family.

I call her a winner.

Reality check: Being passed is part of the race
December 10, 1997

I first noticed the pain in my right shoulder at work. I wasn't in agony, but it was enough to make me wonder: "What have I done to myself this time?"

I contemplated the onset of arthritis: perhaps a muscle strain while changing a tire. Then it dawned on me that I had spent the previous evening tossing a football around with my 10-year-old son, Evan, who has suddenly blossomed into a football fanatic. And, thus the story.

I can recall a time when I began to face both a changing voice and an interest in besting my dad in anything I could. He was the standard from which I measured my strength. As in Evan's case with me, I challenged my dad to an arm- wrestle whenever I could, and dreamed of the day I'd rap his freckled knuckles on the tabletop. It's a natural rite of passage in a boy's life.

I remember finally beating my dad, although I had to have been nearly 20 before I finally got the job done. It struck me as odd then that I wasn't all that happy to win. I guess I finally experienced a change that I didn't enjoy all that much.

Surely some of the worst parts of life's race, and some of its best, has to be the challenge of watching a son pass you by. Time is taking its toll.

It's been nearly seven years since I found myself in an Indianapolis knee surgeon's office. The mostly one-sided conversation went something like this:

"Let me guess," the doctor said. "You're about 35, and you were playing basketball with kids who were about 16, right?"

'Well, yeah, but…."

"You were about to say," he interrupted, "that this whole thing was someone else's fault. You're in the best shape of your life, right?"

"Well, yeah, but…"

"We see guys like you in here all the time," he added with an avaricious grin. "That's how I make a nice living."

I have reached an age when athletic supporters have given way to knee braces, and tennis elbow is creeping suspiciously into other body parts. I'm positive that I will require thumb-joint replacement surgery long before I master my boy's video football game. The old jump shot is falling a little short, and my chest is headed south for the winter too.

In September we took my son to run in the annual "Children's Classic" at Union Hospital. I first began running with him there when he was just 6, just to make sure that he didn't wander off down a side street. Over the years I just kept jogging along with him, most often to push him a little to keep him going. It's become a fall tradition now.

It has also become increasingly difficult to beat him. This year he finished near the front of the pack, and sadly enough, in front of me.

I paid him our modest dollar wager after I had enough breath to get my hand in a pocket. The little mercenary promptly asked me if we could up the ante next year.

I vaguely remember hearing someone say as I rounded the last corner toward the hospital—somehow it was appropriate that I was running near the emergency room—"You're the first adult to come along so far."

Well, just wait until next year. I'm sure that I can do much worse.

'Barnburner' turns game back to its older days
February 4, 1998

If you attend high school basketball games long enough, you'll have the opportunity to learn all kinds of new words. I just happened to have heard an old one last Friday that merits this story.

As is most often the case, I often wander up the road to the local high school to take in a game, one in which the home team managed a four-point overtime win over a county rival, and I heard the game described more than once as a "barnburner."

I've used that word a few times myself, and it doesn't take a wizard to figure out that it probably dates back to the days when Indiana's high school gyms were little more than barns heated by coal stoves. Sportswriter Bob Williams addresses the phrase in his book, "Hoosier Hysteria," published in 1982.

The game has changed considerably since the years before the "Great War," and Williams pointed out that Wingate is probably the place that can lay claim to coining the phrase around that time.

For several years Wingate's Spartans were the dominant basketball team in the state. Nestled in the northwestern-most corner of Montgomery County, the tiny high school in the town of about 400 won back-to-back state titles in 1913 and 1914, and for a good while had no gym at all, eventually earning the nickname of the "gymless wonders."

Wonders they were. The 1912-1913 squad, led by the legendary Homer Stonebraker, knocked off South Bend Central 14-13 for the state crown, but it took five two-minute overtime periods to do it. Wingate had 12 boys enrolled in the school at the time, and seven of them played on the basketball team.

Wingate's knickered look was actually a uniform comprised of baseball pants, knee-length socks, and a sweatshirt. To my knowledge, none of the apparel carried the logo of a major shoe manufacturer.

The Spartans must have been a formidable club. They steamrolled local competition, often with point totals that defy the age. They crushed Hillsboro 108-8, scored 85 on Cayuga, and 75 on Waveland. They took out Whiting, Rochester, Indianapolis Manual, and Lafayette Jefferson en route to the state championship game. The finals were in Bloomington in those days, and Coach Jesse Wood took his team there on a Monon train.

The tournament was larger the next season, and Wingate had a new coach, Leonard Lehman. Seventy-six games were played in four gymnasiums at Indiana University that year, and the Spartans played six of them in two days, destroying Anderson 36-8 for the title. It's interesting to note that Wingate played its closest game in the tournament against Clinton. The 17-13 victory came on the heels of a 24-1 win over archrival Crawfordsville.

Wingate started a basketball program in 1907, but didn't have a gym until 1915. The barn-like structure was built as a homage to the two-time champs, and remained in use until the early 1950s. It had seating on one side, and held 187 people. Showers weren't available for 10 years, so players cleaned up by taking turns stepping into a large galvanized washtub.

Before their new gym was built, the team rented a local livery stable at $3 a practice, or $6 a game. The players and coaches often hitched up horses or crammed into Model Ts to drive the six miles eastward across Coal Creek to play in neighboring New Richmond.

One of the most amazing facts about this tale is that Wingate's success was no passing fancy, nor was it in the rest of Montgomery County. Despite the fact that Wingate and Crawfordsville—the Athenians were winners of the first state tourney in 1911—had been suspended for the 1920 season by the IHSAA, both schools were invited to the National Scholastic Tournament at the University of Chicago.

After downing teams from Iowa, Ohio, and Illinois, the Spartans, led by Stonebraker's heir apparent, Alonzo Goldsberry, defeated their county foes 21- 16 in the title game. A backyard rivalry led to a national championship.

Williams never really defines why the word means a "nip-and-tuck struggle," but Unionville, another small town, this one just north of Bloomington in Monroe County, may lay claim to the truest of barnburners. Like Wingate, the Arrows didn't have a decent gym to call their own. In 1924, a barn-like gym was built, and Unionville used it for basketball in some way or another until 1961, when it burned to the ground. According to writer Donald Hamilton, the Arrows scored 110 points in a game just a few days before the fire. After the fire, school officials found a twisted and melted rim, had it mounted, and packed it off to the Indiana Basketball Hall of Fame.

Regardless of what it's called, a game that goes down to the wire, or ends in a heartbeat, is decided by a last-second shot, or burns the barn, must be a good one: the best kind.

I have a few friends who can remember the days of playing in gyms heated by stoves. One even told me that it was a strategy in those days to nudge an opponent into one of the stoves while an official was preoccupied.

It sounds like more ended up being burned in those days than just barns.

Longing for days of 'Choo-Choo' and 'New Boy'
February 18, 1998

If you make the morning rounds in Brazil on most days, you'll probably run into Paul Sneddon. It may be at the local Hardees, or at Wal-Mart, but you'll see him.

And, if you want to stop and talk, the conversation sooner than later will be about basketball.

Sneddon, Van Buren High School, Class of 1953, enjoys the retired life, a good cup of coffee, and high school basketball, but not necessarily in that order. Paul's memories take him back through almost 50 years of prep hoops to the days when his Blue Devils played the likes of the Reelsville Indians and the Coal City Colts.

One of the things that I picked up after a few minutes with Paul is his sense of regret that we no longer give our favorite players nicknames. Our local high school heroes may have longer shorts, better shoes, and a variety of haircuts and hair colors, but there aren't many who have nicknames. At one time a unique moniker was a standard piece of equipment.

Sneddon remembers the days of Jim "Chub" Withers, who with "New Boy" Bob Dixon, played on the 1950 Blue Devils team. Why those names?

"Well, Chub wasn't fat, but he was stocky-built, so everybody just called him Chub, see. He was a good ballplayer too. Now New Boy, he moved into Knightsville, and since he was a new boy in our school, that's how he got his name. Those names just stuck with them for years," Paul said.

Another player Paul recalled was Brazil's "Choo-Choo" Grissom. "He ran the ball in football like a choo-choo train, and the name just stayed with him for basketball. He was on the varsity team as a sophomore in 1959, and he was on their 1961 team that won the Valley [Wabash Valley Tournament]," Paul said.

Sneddon had reason to remember Grissom well. Brazil went to the semi- state tournament in '59, but only after getting past Van Buren's excellent 21-1 team at the sectional level. The Blue Devils had lost only to Brownsburg that year in a Valley game.

After the loss, Paul cheered for what would be a remarkable Red Devils squad. The team had won only a half dozen games prior to the sectional win over Van Buren at the old Spencer gymnasium.

"Me and some other guys all drove down to Spencer in a real big snow—six or seven inches—for that game," Paul said. "We got there, and it had just started. Brazil got up six or ten points in the first half, but then things really tightened up."

With less than a minute left in the game, and Van Buren up by a point, Brazil's Russell Barnett tipped in a rebound basket. The victorious Red Devils eventually traveled to the "Sweet Sixteen" with their losing record, beating Wiley in the regional tournament, avenging a huge regular season loss to the Red Streaks. Brazil's run ended in a loss to New Albany, a Final Four team.

"I remember so many of us were such fans," Sneddon added. 'A friend of ours was a red-hot fan then, and he drove to that game [the '59 sectional] straight from the Greencastle stockyards, where he worked. Boy, you could tell right away that he hadn't been able to clean up before he got there too."

His memory crisp with details, Paul and his pals talk over the daily basketball headlines each morning. He thought it interesting that two of the boys who played on the '50 Van Buren squad were guard Herb Rissler and big center Jack Grantham. Years later they remain teammates as professors at Indiana State University.

"Us guys sit around at Hardees and talk about basketball. We've been talkin' about Sharpie [Howard

Sharpe] this week and his 759 victories. That's a lot of wins," Paul said.

With that, Sneddon recalled another nickname and another tale. "Oh, if I had the time, I could remember more, but I do remember 'Varsity' Bob Black. When he was on the JV, he kept saying, 'I'm good enough to be on the varsity.' So, we just called him 'Varsity.' He eventually made it too, but he was just a sophomore then. We had a lot of fun in those days," Paul said.

He can tell you all about it too. All you have to do is ask.

Class changes can't compare to rule changes
March 15, 1998

For all that's been said about the sanctity of Indiana High School basketball as its first year with a class system nears an end, the game itself hasn't significantly changed this season.

Despite what some see as the heresy of four classes and the end of traditional tournament rivalries, the most significant alterations to basketball through the years have come through rule changes. The fact is that basketball isn't the same game it was when the first state tournament began in 1911.

That was made clear to me as I listened to an interview veteran broadcaster Darl Wible included in his four-CD collection of classic Wabash Valley and Vigo County games released just a few months ago. The set was co-produced by the WTHI stations and Terre Haute First National Bank. Conducted in February 1952, the 6-minute interview was with David Glascock, who coached the very first IHSAA champion 87 years ago. His Crawfordsville Athenians claimed the title by winning four games in two days at Bloomington.

Glascock noted that basketball before World War I was unique. They played 20-minute halves in those days, no one dribbled the ball, and they played with four-man offenses and defenses. Although I'm not exactly sure what they were, Glascock also said that he used a "floating center," and a "back guard." The guard never crossed the center of the floor, except to steal the ball.

The Athenians proved that winning a state tournament back then took stamina. The Athenians played and won three games in just nine hours at the old Assembly Hall, which had a capacity of about 1,200. The seven-man squad spent its time between games in a fraternity house and was fed steaks in bed.

Glascock also mentioned that he had always felt Sloan's Liniment helped his team win the state crown. Apparently someone spilled a bottle of the stuff on the players' uniforms, and Glascock said that his boys kept moving just to keep from burning up.

I went to an interesting source to find major rule changes in Indiana basketball. Max Knight's "Somebody Stole the Pea Out of My Whistle" (Guild Press of Indiana, 1995) is a delightful series of stories about officiating in the game's "golden years." In it, veteran referee Don McBride said that the most significant rule change in high school basketball came in 1938. It was the adoption of the 10-second backcourt rule.

"Prior to that time a player could hold the ball at his end of the court an entire quarter if no defensive player came after him. There were games when a player receiving the ball would place it on the floor and sit down on it until he was challenged," McBride said.

The size of gym floors during that era was also interesting. There were no rules in those days dictating gym floor width or length. Most gyms were fairly small and so were the floors in them. Most were usually at least 42 feet wide, but some were even shorter than the 64-foot court at Fountain City.

In another interesting section, McBride included what he called "Ridiculous Rules." For instance, a 1913 rule said that if a referee determined that a player was face guarding his opponent, the ref could whistle a foul despite no contact being made.

A 1920 ruling stated that a player could not re-enter a game more than once. That regulation lasted until 1944. Another interesting change came in 1937. It limited the number of overtimes to two. After that, the game would be called a tie. After just one year, sudden death was introduced, and that rule stood until 1961.

In 1943, a new regulation read that a player who was fouled by more than one opponent at the same time could receive a free throw for each foul. That rule lasted only one year.

According to McBride, "the dumbest rule change in history" was the 1983 adoption of the alternating possession for jump balls. He claims the rule often fails to reward teams for good defense and "simply does not make sense." As a coach, I never cared for it either.

The oft-proposed change that may have the most impact in quite some time comes from those who continue to push for a 30-or 40-second shot clock.

The game in Indiana will withstand the tinkering of those who support classes, but I hope I never see a shot clock in an Indiana high school gymnasium.

Author finds hoop heaven in 'Hickory'
October 14, 1998

I found basketball heaven this summer. It's in eastern Indiana, just off Interstate 70. It doesn't look like much these days, despite a fresh coat of paint applied about 12 years ago. Yet, walking into the old Knightstown gym invokes a feeling that I can't imagine being felt elsewhere.

Knightstown is where the motion picture "Hoosiers" was filmed in 1986. Despite the fact that the gym quietly creeps once again toward disrepair, there's more to it than meets the eye.

I took my family to the pleasant little town a few months ago. We spent some time just up the road at the Indiana High School Basketball Hall of Fame in New Castle, and I took a chance that we'd get through a chained door to see hallowed ground.

The gym was locked when we pulled past it on a smoldering hot July afternoon. We wandered to every door and window, hoping that someone could let us in, but it was obvious that no one was inside. We finally rustled up a friendly secretary who was hibernating in her air conditioning at the grade school across the street, and she informed us that the local school corporation doesn't even own the old place anymore.

She told me that the town owned it, mentioned that I might be able to look up Ed Somebody who might have a key. Ed might have even been at home, if I could have found my way to his house. But that would have required finding a certain gas station whose attendant might be able to tell me exactly where Ed lived.

We settled instead for sitting a while on the decrepit steps of the gym's crumbling front entrance under the shade of an ancient pine. It seemed as if our pilgrimage was over, that is until we saw a little boy, shorts dangling to the tips of his hightops, walking up the street with a smooth playground basketball tucked under his arm.

Despite the heat, a devout Knightstown mom, who, like Ed, had a key and helped run an occasional open gym for grade schoolers, pulled her van to the curb a few minutes later.

I felt I needed to explain why my family wanted to get inside the musty old fossil, but she said there wasn't a need for an explanation. She's seen it before: people who for some odd reason are as attracted to "Hickory High" as Joe Jackson was to his "Field of Dreams" in Iowa.

My son and I shot around awhile with a borrowed ball, and the Lunsford family took the tour, even down to the scruffy subterranean locker rooms, dimly lit by a few solitary bulbs. When done, we sat for a while in the pock-marked bleachers and soaked in the heat of the day and the wonderful simplicity of the place.

As in the film's closing scene, a huge team photo of the mythical state champion Huskers sits above the main entrance of the gym. The faces stare out at a place that has seen its better days, a place that once housed its own glory as the Knightstown five faced the Middletown Cossacks or the Mooreland Bobcats.

Barbara Hershey, as Myra Fleener, was right. We can take comfort in the fact that some things never change.

Photograph recalls flood of memories
October 26, 1998

I found a piece of the past last week as I explored an old trunk in my living room. Among the bundles of tax receipts, leaf collections, and record albums was a single newspaper clipping, a photograph.

The photo of the 11 young girls has yellowed. The coach standing among their "we're number one" forefingers is a skinnier, longer-haired version of me. The first team I coached, a bunch of eighth-grade over-achievers, had won the county championship tournament.

I don't expect many readers will care about that team, or about my coaching career, one reason I have never written about the latter. Yet that crumbling picture exemplifies what was best about coaching for 14 years and why it was so difficult to give up.

I've lost track of many of the kids on that first team, and I know it won't be long before several of their children will be walking into my high school classroom. When I reach a third generation — those players' grandkids — I think I should be walking out of the classroom for good.

That first group of mine had no real star. Most of the kids were hard workers who giggled their way through practice and stayed later than they had to. Our old crackerbox of a gym lost out to the wrecking ball just a few years later. Its floor had died in places and we swept bits of the crumbling ceiling off to the edges before we started each night.

Their seventh-grade year had been a disaster, but for some inexplicable reason, they believed in me, and in themselves, and we ended up winning 11 of 13 games, most by scores as close as that championship game, 19-16.

It has been nearly six seasons since I gave up coaching, almost 18 since I began with no experience at the varsity level, and I still run into folks who call me "coach." I stopped correcting them a while ago because it's a title of which I'll never tire.

The object lesson here is not about teamwork or dedication or believing in one's self or one's coach. It's not even about the value of memories. The lesson comes from the one player on that team who didn't play much, an often sleepy, freckled red head named Joyce Spencer.

When the nets had been cut, the lights turned off, and the celebration over, Joyce came to me, a few tears running down her cheeks. I thought she was upset, because as the last player off the bench for me, she hadn't gotten to play a single minute that night.

"Thanks for letting me play this year, Coach," she blurted out.

I just stood there, dumbfounded by how gracious she was.

She added, "It was nice to just be on the team. Thanks."

Joyce, I don't think I told you then, but thank you.

Broadcasting sounds easy, but don't let ears fool you
November 25, 1998

When I was a kid I used to stay up at night and listen to the old Marathon Radio Network. It was the ABA days of Mel Daniels and Roger Brown, and Joe McConnell called Indiana Pacers' games from Oakland and Salt Lake City.

McConnell made play-by-play sound easy. So did Jack Buck. Often I would fall asleep listening to him do Cardinals' games from the West Coast, the light of my brother's old Clarion receiver illuminating our bedroom with its amber glow.

My mom knew it was late, but I guess she figured that despite the hour on school nights, there was something inherently good about a boy listening to a game on the radio. I appreciated her letting me have those "Radio Days."

Another broadcaster who always made it sound easy to me was Jim Jerome. He and his partner, Charlie Bemis, became friends of mine while I was still coaching. Jim called games for WAXI out of Rockville, and he was one of the best around for more than 40 years. Jerome hosted a Saturday morning talk show too. His guests were mostly coaches who shoveled in free eggs and toast while they lied to each other about how bad their teams were. Jim always managed to make my teams sound a little better than they actually were, and he continued to put in all those years in the business because he loves kids and high school basketball.

A few weeks ago, I found myself at the Banks of the Wabash girls tournament at Riverton Parke, a little anxious to get an early-season basketball fix. I hadn't been there five minutes when Jim's successor at WAXI, Jimmy Beasley, waved me over and explained that his partner for the evening hadn't showed up. He wanted me to fill in for a while. I had helped Jerome a few times at a sectional or weekend boys game years ago, so I at least knew how to put on a headset.

But those few minutes turned into over three hours and two full games. Yet, I have to admit, I had fun. Whether Beasley, or the folks who listened enjoyed it, is another matter.

Doing those games reinforced what I found out years ago: sports broadcasting may sound easy, but it really isn't. Jimmy, like Jim and Charlie, spent much of the night sweating bullets as he fiddled with dials, wires, and microphones. He kept a scorebook, watched four rosters to learn names, listened to someone back at the station out of one ear, and to me out of the other. He was still packing his gear when the custodians began to sweep up.

My job as a "color commentator" was pretty simple. I just watched the game, waited for Beasley to take a breath, and piped in with my opinion about a full-court press or timely substitution. It took a few minutes to get over the initial terror of staring down my nose at a live microphone, but I eventually relaxed.

What was debilitating was that often Jimmy would wander away from me to handle some chore with a cable or antenna. He urged me to blab while he chatted with some passer-by, paid for popcorn, or burrowed around in a canvas bag of assorted tools and tape. To a novice announcer, the Jeromes and Beasleys are life-support systems. When Jimmy bravely asked me to "bring us back" from a commercial break, it took a few decades of embarrassed silence before I caught on to what he was saying. After that, I made him swear that he would not ask me to do play-by-play, or I'd drop the mike and run.

If Jimmy needs a hand again, I'll be happy to help. And, now that I'm an experienced radio personality, I want to pass the most valuable piece of advice I know to those contemplating a career in the sportscasting business: Go to the bathroom before the game starts.

Second Quarter
Fall 1999-Winter 2001

Wait just a minute while I get my list…
October 12, 1999

It suddenly came to me the other day that I'm one of those pathetically organized people who lives his life through a series of notes and plans scribbled on pads and detailed in notebooks.

It's common knowledge that I often begin to make a new list before I finish an old one: I'm a chain-lister. At one time, I was a three-list-a-day man. Like the poor chump in an old Gary Larson cartoon, I envision a time when I'll need to plaster a huge note to my bedroom wall at bedtime just to remind myself that the pants go on before the shoes each morning.

These past few months have been a real joy to me and to the others who share in my sickness. One of the trends I've noticed in these waning days of the millennium has been our collective desire to see things listed: The greatest ballplayers; the best actors; the most important inventions.

Time magazine has been working toward naming its "Man of the Century" for a good while; ESPN has its "Sports Century;" Major League Baseball will soon announce its "All Century Team." Professional basketball beat everybody to the punch; the NBA named its 50 greatest players a year ago.

As it enters its fourth year, this column is supposed to be primarily occupied with basketball, and I think that fact itself suggests that a few lists are appropriate. When I think about the game, especially the high school variety, I believe there's a great deal more to like than dislike. For instance, I like old gymnasiums; the creaky, dusty, dark and nostalgic ones—the kind that will never be built again. Like the old baseball parks that now face the wrecking ball in Detroit and Boston, they may be too small or need a coat of paint, but they'll be missed, and most often, we'll realize that fact after it's too late to do anything about it.

I like to hear kids sing the national anthem before ball games. There's something strangely reassuring about that. I like coaches who coach, players who work hard, and cheerleaders who truly care about what's going on in the game.

I like it when little kids sit behind the team benches, dreaming, perhaps, that someday they'll be on it. I like high school bands, "On Wisconsin," full-court presses, and good popcorn.

I like to sit near the old-timers: the ones in cardigans who played as boys or at one time coached them. They still X and 0, but more than that, they use the games as vehicles to their pasts. They remember an age when warm-ups were wool, trunks were satin, and dribbling around dead spots in warped floors was routine. They still treat each game as both reunion and renewal.

I like good free throw shooting, cross-county rivalries, and warm gyms on cold nights. I like to find the player who's always looking for the open man, and I love to listen to games on the radio. I like upsets, and I like to wander past team photos from the old days mounted on the gym walls, the rows of skinny legs and bony chests standing there mute and proud.

There's a few things I can't like. I don't care for coaches who perform for the crowd; cheerleaders who are more concerned about their hair than the score; kids who run up and down the bleachers dripping a variety of goos on my jacket; lazy players; black athletic socks; and chest-thumping.

I hate taunting and ballhogs; cold gyms and warm cokes. I don't like faking the charge, and I cheer when whiners lose; I still can't understand why the hook shot and jump ball are dead.

The listing of lists about basketball is a limitless leisure. There are long lists—the best games I've ever seen. There are short lists—profound things Dennis Rodman has said. There are memorable lists—Stacey Toran's 60-footer at the buzzer in the 1980 state finals. There are favorite lists—Mount and Bird and the Big 0.

In his classic travelogue, "Blue Highways," William Least Heat Moon wrote about one evening on the road that was "one of those sweet moments in life that I'll take to the grave."

A simple game with a simple goal has given me many of those moments. I could make a list...

******Author's Note: The words by William Least Heat Moon in this column are repeated in an "Off Season" story I wrote six years later.***

There's plenty in sports world to feel warm and fuzzy about
November 24, 1999

I had a fellow ask me the other day if I had been hired by this newspaper to specifically write with only a positive spin, to try to give as many of the readers as possible the "warm and fuzzies."

He wasn't saying it as a compliment.

The writing process isn't too complicated for me. I write my column, get it to the sports desk painfully close to deadline, and hope that it ends up in print. I've never been ordered to write about any particular person, place, or thing that wasn't my choice. So far, everything I've hashed out has ended up on the sports page for the readers' perusal whether they've liked it or not.

As to my sarcastic friend, I can only give him the raspberry. I usually write positively about positive people because I'm tired of being bombarded by negative stories about negative people. I feel many of my column-writing colleagues feel much the same way. I don't think that I'm alone when I say that the typical reader is disgusted by the endless parade of newspaper stories about this professional athlete's recent arrest for reckless driving, that college star awaiting a chance to play again after violating his probation, or those dozen or so big-name green-mongers who continue to hold out for ridiculously high renegotiated contracts. I read just the other day that a typical seat at a New York Knicks game costs $86…

The sports pages these days often read like police rap sheets. It may be the way of the world, but I don't have to write about the thieves and thugs who hide themselves behind the ability to shoot the 3-pointer or run a sideline pass route. As a matter of fact, I'm proud that I don't have to resort to it.

One player that I would like to read more about, however, is Kristin Coletti, a senior at South Vermillion High School. Coletti should be pretty easy to spot on the basketball floor because she's the one with the huge brace strapped over her reconstructed knee.

"Kristin is a never-quit athlete," said Wildcats Coach Tim Terry. "She's got a big heart, and she gives 100 percent in practice, not just games. She's the kind of kid who gets in a game and just goes after it." Terry illustrated the point: "A lot of people don't really realize just how little Kristin is—she's so small, but she ended up just a couple of rebounds shy of being our rebounding leader last year. That proves to me how much courage she really has."

Coletti's cross-country coach, Mike Costello, must have had a vision when I called him for information about high-performing, low-whining athletes.

"Kristin Coletti," he offered before I had mentioned her name. "She's one of those kids who comes along just a few times in a coach's career. She's what high school sports should be about."

Costello was upset when Coletti ripped her ACL late last winter, but knew that despite her missing much of the track season in the spring because of the surgery, she'd be back running this fall.

"She's a leader, doesn't worry about individual stats, and has a great work ethic. It's hard to describe to people who may not be associated with sports, but 'gutsy' is the word I use when I describe her. I don't suppose that I should have used that word in a letter of recommendation that I just wrote for her, but that's what she is."

Kristin will probably never play basketball in the WNBA or run cross-country for a major college, but I don't think I'll ever read about her in the police blotter or court news either She simply reminds me of an old Pete Seeger lyric: "Do-so is more important than say-so."

For about $83 less than a Knicks' ticket, you can see her prove it this winter.

Advice from Dr. Jack still rings true
December 8, 1999

Watching Jack Ramsay's basketball commentary on ESPN one morning a few weeks ago jogged a bit of memory for me.

Eleven years ago I was working at Billy Keller's Indiana Pacers' summer basketball camp at Rose-Hulman. One of the perks of coaching at the camp, besides watching Keller enthusiastically work with the kids, was a visit from Ramsay, who was then the head coach in Indianapolis. It's the same Ramsay who guided Bill Walton's Portland Trailblazers to the NBA championship in 1977.

I had an extra pass for the clinic, so I invited Bobby Cleghorn, a former coach himself, to go over to hear Ramsay's discussion of athletic conditioning. From previous experience at coaching clinics, I expected Ramsay to do very little moving and a lot of talking.

When conditioning is the topic of conversation, most coaches normally get their exercise by blowing a whistle while a few underlings lose their lunch showing how it's done. After all, a good many coaches I'd known through the years had spent as much time in the buffet line as on the practice floor.

But Ramsay surprised me. We met in one of Rose-Hulman's science lecture halls, and the spry, wiry coach, who had to be nearing his mid-60s by then, walked briskly into the room and leaped on an elevated table that had to be three feet off the ground. He then proceeded to explain stretching exercises and the science of jump-training while he paced across the table like a caged cougar, all the while jabbing an enthusiastic finger in the air to emphasize his points.

Ramsay was planning to run in a triathlon a few days later, and he placed a tremendous emphasis on stretching muscles and proper diets as keys to being in peak physical condition. If I recall correctly, Ramsay's chat sent Bobby and me on a brief guilt trip. We still had the grease stains on our shirts from the jumbo sausage and extra cheese pizza we'd wolfed down a few minutes before heading to Rose. I don't think that either of us could have touched our toes to save our lives that night, yet there was a guy twice our age doing chin-ups on the door frame. We at least tried to suck in our guts.

When he had finished, Ramsay exited the room like a well-executed fast break stopping long enough to crush a few hands with his hearty grip. At the time, I was certain that he was off to do a few thousand push-ups before his bedtime spinach shake.

The story really doesn't end there. I've been impressed with Ramsay ever since that brief meeting, not for the championship ring he wore, or even the strong conviction he held for strictly adhering to a regimen of fresh fruits and vegetables. He's a walking juicer commercial, and I'd applaud him yet if I didn't have a cream-filled donut in my hand. Ramsay is a man of conviction. He's old-school; he tends to think and believe that basketball isn't just something that makes one money; it builds character. I came to believe that after hearing him speak that night and after reading a list of tenants that he published years ago.

The list is called "Jack Ramsay's Dozen List of Absolutes in Coaching," and it's something that every basketball coach from grade school to the professional ranks should read and promote with his or her players. Here it is.

1. Basketball, like every other sport, is predicated on the execution of fundamentals.

2. The coach is the teacher; his subject is the fundamentals.

3. The highest level of achievement is attained by teams with the best conditioned players.

4. Even the greatest players have a level of improvement to achieve.

5. Even the greatest players accept coaching and value the need for discipline and the order that it brings to a team.

6. Winning is more related to good defense than good offense.

7. Breakdown drills, under simulated conditions, are essential to team success.

8. Teams that play together beat those with superior players who play more as individuals.

9. There are no physical limits to individual achievement.

10. Although the game has become more sophisticated, simpler is better in developing and teaching a system of play.

11. Players draw confidence from a poised, alert coach who anticipates changing game conditions.

12. Teams that never concede defeat can accomplish incredible victories.

Ramsay hasn't tackled life in his 70s with high fiber brownies and offers to appear in denture adhesive commercials. He's a Hall of Famer, does game analysis for NBA Today, and is in his eighth season as the color man for the Miami Heat broadcasts. He's still preaching a gospel, that although as old as he is, will still work. It's too bad that so few are listening.

It seems to me that he has even more work to do now. I imagine he has the energy for it too.

Reminiscing about Mount, Keller, and Roy
February 2, 2000

It may have been the falling snow or the cardinals at my feeders; it may have been the Purdue-Indiana game on the television and the warm chair from which I watched it all, but I've been reminiscing lately about a time that means more to me now than it did years ago.

Writers and readers alike generally use the word nostalgia almost condescendingly, as if it is an affliction of the aged and infirm. I don't agree. As I watched the Boilermakers beat the Hoosiers two Saturdays ago, it was the nostalgic memories that transformed me into a 12-year-old kid again.

My Grandfather Roy knew absolutely nothing about sports. The only time I ever saw him with a basketball in his hands came when my ball rolled away from my backyard goal and toward his garden. He knew the names of few athletes and had no interest whatsoever in the sports pages. After a lifetime of manual labor, he thought that professional sports were rather silly. To him, playing a game wasn't a very good way to support a family. But on a good many snowy January afternoons, I could be found stretched out in front of my grandfather's old black and white Zenith console watching Purdue basketball on Channel 4, and my grandfather, at least for a little while, was transformed into a fan.

After my grandmother passed, I spent more time with my granddad than I ever had, which is difficult to imagine since we were fishing pals long before I ever took notice of basketball. His strawberries lay just a few feet from my worn dirt arena, his house a hundred yards or so from my back porch.

On nearly every winter Saturday afternoon, and in the evenings on a few weekdays a month, I'd shuffle up his driveway, plow through the backdoor into his kitchen, and after a thorough raid on his refrigerator, plop myself in front of his TV. He'd make a single cup of instant coffee straight from his hot water tap, then join me in cheering from his recliner.

In those days, Rick Mount and Billy Keller were leading the Boilers through the Big Ten Conference, while George King was doing the coaching. Those were the days of pure jump shooters, and I now wonder what kind of unimaginable numbers would have been recorded by gunners like Mount and Pete Maravich had they been able to play four years instead of three, and had the three-point shot been around.

My grandpa became a great fan of "The Rocket," in particular. In fact, since the only games he tended to watch besides those starring the real Mount were the private ones I regularly held in my backyard, he gave me the nickname too. Believe me, a little blonde hair was our only shared resemblance.

It was Mount's last-second, overtime heroics against Marquette in the NCAA regional final that eventually prodded a few enthusiastic fans to swipe his life-sized sign near Lebanon—his hometown—and install it 30 miles away at West Lafayette. My particular homage to the fabled star came by wearing a faded old gold Purdue sweatshirt and Converse high tops everywhere I could. I even hung on to my crewcut for a while.

In 1969, the Boilers advanced all the way to the NCAA title game against UCLA. I remember how badly I wanted them to win, and how badly Lew Alcindor and John Wooden crushed them. The Bruins "held" Mount to 28 points, and Purdue never made it a very close game.

Watching the Boilermakers in those days, minus Gene Keady's scowl, the Big Ten post-season tournament, and the dunk shot—Alcindor's dominance led it to be outlawed—was an experience. Mackey Arena was still new, and besides Mount, who was just a junior, and Keller, a scrappy, ball-handling wizard, the Boilers had Herm Gilliam (actually their second leading scorer), forward George Faerber, and a 7-footer named Chuck Bavis. Larry Weatherford was just a sophomore on the 1969 team too, and he eventually joined Keller, Gilliam, and, of course, Mount, by scoring over 1,000 points in his career. Mount, by the way, finished with over 2,300.

After the Boilers faltered against UCLA, and Mount graduated a year later, we spent our Saturdays with NBC, Notre Dame and Austin Carr, who scored even more points a game than Mount did.

Years later, long after my grandfather had died, I was able to meet Mount as he sold athletic equipment, and Keller at his summer camp. I tried as best I could to relate to them, as they autographed a book or program, the story of how much time I'd spend with my grandfather watching them tackle Wisconsin or Minnesota as we snacked on canned soup and crackers.

I have said it time and time again, and apparently some readers agree, that there's something missing from sports that used to be there. It's difficult to describe, but I admired Mount and Keller, and I feel my granddad did too, not because of the money that they both eventually made playing in the old ABA, but because they seemed to love what they were doing and worked so hard at it.

I don't follow the Boilers very much these days, and I think it's because I just can't seem to see them in the same way I once did. I guess it was the company I kept too.

According to essayist Scott Russell Sanders, nostalgia is a word coined in 1688 as a medical term. It seems its creators were interested in describing the condition we now call homesickness. Sanders also explained that the Greek roots of the word literally mean "return pain."

In the case of Rocket Rick and those Saturday afternoon games with my grandfather, nostalgia doesn't hurt at all.

Times change for Clinton man, but not memories
February 15, 2000

Bud McCammon is one of those people who keeps everything. The walls of his office are choked with framed photos and memorabilia; his scrapbooks and old high school yearbooks lay open on a desk overcrowded with papers and files. But of all the things he's collected over the years, the memories of the good times a half century ago are perhaps the most important to him.

An administrator for the Vermillion County Health Department, McCammon lives just a stone's throw from his cubby-holed office near the county hospital where he works with his wife, Martha. As he puts it, "I'm past retirement age, so I have nothing to do but go to ball games. Basketball is just my thing, I guess."

That's a king-sized understatement. He's currently working to organize a special team reunion in early March. It was 50 years ago next month that as a hustling, junior guard, McCammon helped his Clinton Wildcats make a memorable run for basketball glory. That run came to end only after the Wildcats had reached the Indianapolis Semistate at Hinkle Fieldhouse, dropping a 67-60 decision to Rushville.

McCammon knows he's biased, but feels the times in which he grew up were special, as was the brand of basketball played in those days.

"You know, as a player, we were treated so well. There wasn't a stranger out there; everyone was proud," McCammon said. "People took basketball very personally then; it was their town. We had great rivalries then too, and when we came back from the regional they put us all on a fire truck and drove us around. The Indianapolis newspaper even came over to talk to us, but what were we going to say, just a bunch of 17-year-old kids?"

McCammon was not originally from Clinton. He transferred from Garfield as a freshman and still displays his McLean eighth-grade team photo on his wall. His playing career got its start in much the same way as other youngsters in those days.

"I used to live near 12 Points, and we used to play ball in the back alleys then. There was one old-timer—he was about 40 or 45, but that was old to us—who used to travel the alleys just to play against us kids. We even played in Willard Kehrt's basement with a volleyball," he said.

McCammon played a year of freshman ball at Clinton before moving up to the varsity team under Coach Robert Burton. He made a point to mention that he felt he was taught to play by two of the best coaches in the area: Kehrt and Burton, while Howard Sharpe was surely in their company.

"They all taught fundamentals," McCammon said of the legendary coaches. "Our team at Clinton was fundamentally sound. That's the way Mr. Burton taught us. No one person was outstanding; everybody contributed. I think you could have taken about any five of us that year and not lose a whole lot."

The 1949-50 Wildcats finished at 19-11, but all of those losses came to quality teams, including Garfield, Sullivan, Wiley, Brazil, Gerstmeyer, and Greencastle. Clinton advanced to within a game of the Wabash Valley Tournament title that year too, losing only to champion Glenn in the semi-final. By the time the Wildcats headed into the post-season, they had a full head of steam. "We played a lot of zones then; we weren't real big," he said. "Our biggest player was Albert Gilmore, and he was only about 6-2. Mr. Burton always emphasized blocking out, and everybody except one of us would be crashing the boards," McCammon said.

The Wildcats took out Hillsdale, Cayuga, Rosedale, and Rockville in the Sectional round, then defeated Richland Township before gaining revenge against Greencastle 57-50 in the Regional championship game.

Joining McCammon as Wildcats guards were Jim Edler, Don Gilman, Louis Sasso, and Jim "Beenix"

Reeder. The forwards were Mike Dick, Bill "Boogie" Rayce, Max Call, David Lindsey, and John Lamb. The team's centers were Gene Mack and Albert Gilmore. Lindsey and Call were Clinton's top scorers.

McCammon will never forget the day the Wildcats went to practice at the legendary Hinkle. "If you saw Hoosiers, it was the same feeling," he said. "I remember that it was so cold in that building. We got two hours of practice there, and all you could see when you looked up were those windows all the way at the top. It just scared you."

He also fondly recalls the good times he spent with coaches and teammates around Clinton, and the gym in which he spent his high school career. "We almost always came back from a game and went down to Ninth Street to Antonini's Restaurant, and they'd feed us. When we played in the sectionals, we'd always stay at a parent's house together, and Coach Burton would pick us up in his car."

"[Burton] was a real stickler, even on what we ate. He didn't want us to drink pop. If you screwed up, there was always somebody there to take your place. I remember when I was benched for two games. Albert [Gilmore] and me went to a movie uptown. We had a 10 o'clock curfew, but we stayed until 11. Coach Burton was sitting back behind us and just said, 'Hi, boys,' as we walked out. When we came to practice, we knew there was no use to even dress. He stuck to his guns. You had to respect him for that. It was my fault, and it never happened again," McCammon added.

"Our old gym still looks very good. We had to play in some gyms where you had to plant your feet sideways to get them to fit between the sidelines and the bleachers. Our gym had a stage at one end, and the other end sloped down toward the doors. I remember Jim Reeder broke his arm running into that stage, and a lot of us slid all the way to the entrance when people would track snow onto the floor," he said.

More than most people, McCammon is aware of how important Clinton's rich basketball past has been to his town. The 1947 Wildcats had been to a semi-state too, and 35 Clinton teams made it to the final round of the Wabash Valley. To McCammon's knowledge, no other Clinton team since 1950 made it as far into the state tournament, although the 1968 Wildcats were knocked out in a regional thriller at Bloomington.

"We always had a full house when we played. Why, when we went to the 'Sweet 16,' I think the town was just about empty. I even married a cheerleader, and so did two other guys on the team," McCammon said.

Among McCammon's treasures is a menu from the old Wassell Inn in Terre Haute. Advertising space in his last annual was purchased by the likes of the Duck In Grill and Gillis Pharmacy, businesses that disappeared from Clinton's Main Street long ago.

The times may have changed, but Bud McCammon's memories haven't.

Clearing out the notebook before the snowstorm hits
March 1, 2000

I had an old-timer tell me the other day that he'd seen one sure sign that we'd have a snow storm soon: The sectional tournaments are coming up.

The warm south wind, the harmony of the frogs on the pond below our back hill, and my greening grass this past week have convinced me that winter has lost its grip on us, but since the tourney draw was Sunday, I'll leave my snow shovel near the back door just in case.

Nonetheless, I'm in the process of doing a bit of spring cleaning, and this is to be one of those "I'm-clearing-out-the-notebook" kind of columns. For me, that notebook is a pile of nearly indecipherable scribblings on napkins, receipts, fast-food sacks, and team rosters that bloom on my desk by early March.

For as long as I've written for the Tribune-Star, that pile has been just as reliable as a sectional snowfall. My information-gathering system is the technological equivalent of writing notes to myself on the tops of dusty furniture, but it works well enough. On one note I found the reminder: "Research a few small, local gyms."

I wrote that note while struggling for elbow space in the very last row at the top of Turkey Run High School's cozy gymnasium two Fridays ago. I was having trouble catching glimpses of the Turkey Run-Attica and Rockville-Eminence girls sectional games.

I'll still argue that the IHSAA has mangled the state tournament with its yearly site changes and cross-country drives—just ask Eminence fans—but that claustrophobic, boisterous sweatbox of a gym, and the tight games played that night, were pure pleasure for me.

Some of the best small Indiana gyms have disappeared as the years have flown by. Many survive as community centers or extra elementary school gymnasiums. More have been purchased to serve as warehouses or truckers' garages, and even more have been left to fall into themselves. If only they could talk.

One tiny gym that I remember reading about was in Greene County. The original Newberry gymnasium was built in 1916. After the first state tournament five years earlier, most schools were scrambling to find buildings large enough to hold games; even churches, barns, and opera houses were used. It was quite an event when a small community first opened its gymnasium, and Newberry's was among the first to be designed specifically for basketball, although by today's standards it would be sadly lacking.

According to one account, Newberry fans witnessed an unbelievable game in the winter of 1917 in that gym. The Newberry squad, purportedly nicknamed the River Rats, thumped Worthington 142-2. Newberry's Snowden Hert scored 90 points that night on 45 field goals. L.V. Phillips coached Newberry in those days and later became the commissioner of the IHSAA.

One of the things that has always intrigued me about the gyms of that era was how much they could vary from town to town. Believe it or not, some of the early basketball floors weren't even rectangular, and virtually none of them had a standard length or width. If fans think that winning on the road is a tough task now, imagine what it was like to play away from your home court in those days.

Another one of my notes suggested that I mention the interesting results of a poll taken on a basketball-related Web site: www.indianahoops.com. The question was, "Should the state Legislature get involved with the IHSAA?"

It came as no surprise that only 30 percent of those who responded believed the General Assembly should do just that. A resounding 63 percent thought the

Legislature should pay attention to some of our more pressing concerns.

As a former coach, I can attest to the contrary nature of the IHSAA, and an independent board of review probably should be put in place, but slopping more responsibilities onto the state Legislature's plate would be a poor idea.

Speaking of plates, I had written another note on a photocopied menu. "Talk steak," it read. That note was the result of some editing done to my last column about Bud McCammon, who played for Clinton's 1950 regional championship team.

McCammon is a real pack rat, and one of the things he's kept is an old menu for the Wassel Inn in Terre Haute. In an attempt to wrap up my story with a bit of nostalgia, I mentioned that menu and the fact that a T-bone steak dinner cost a whopping 75 cents. An editor deleted that point, probably because I tend to write novel-length stories.

Finally, I found a note scratched on the back of a team roster that read, "Nick and Jayne." That's not the title of a grade school reader I fondly recall from the days of my youth. My nephew, Nick Nepote, turns 7 on Saturday, and one of my former players—I'll not mention her age—is Jayne Virostko. Both are a bit concerned about my column's photo.

Nick saw the picture as he was hacking his way through the face of a jack-o'-lantern last fall. Old newspapers had been strategically placed over the tabletop, and glancing down to see my photo staring back at him, Nick mentioned that the picture couldn't be of me: I was much more "handsome" than the guy in the paper.

Nick, a bright and attentive young lad, will have an extra birthday gift this spring from his favorite uncle. Jayne, now a veteran math teacher, had the misfortune of being a guard on one of my basketball teams years ago. She now teaches with me and had saved one of my columns a month or so ago and slipped it into my mailbox with a little note attached to it.

"You need a new photo," she said. "You look quite a bit older now than when this one was taken," she caustically added.

I'm writing myself a note right now; Jayne's birthday gift won't be as nice as Nick's.

Basketball is learning how to take the good with the bad
March 16, 2000

As I was slipping on my favorite pair of warm and well-worn blue jeans last Saturday morning, accompanied by the soft cotton socks I yanked on over my bony feet, and the old Browning hunting shirt I inherited from my father's closet, I re-realized that taking the good with the bad is a fact of life.

I could have, for instance, been pulling on a pair of those "hard" jeans, the baggy kind, complete with the legs that can sand the finish off sidewalks and ride uncomfortably below the waistband of your underwear. I could have been suffering through a pair of smelly boot socks or had to settle for a medium-sized "Who Shot J.R.?" T-shirt, one that falls a good 2 inches short of my navel while emphasizing my petite waistline.

Compared to that scenario, those old jeans of mine are a bargain. It's refreshing to apply this good vs. bad principle to basketball, too. I'm the first to admit that I spend a considerable amount of time bad-mouthing what's wrong with the game these days, but actually, there's just as much right with it. Maybe things balance themselves out in the long run.

So it goes as Indiana State's Sycamores head to Salt Lake City for today's showdown against a tough Texas squad in the NCAA tournament. I'm going to take that game as one of those good things; one of the best things. Notre Dame or Virginia fans, by the way, undoubtedly feel that the NCAA selection committee is comprised of nothing but closet fascists, but to ISU fans, sainthood may be in order for the folks who sent them west.

Had the Sycamores been snubbed and reduced to hoping for an NIT bid, I think I could have still applied the principle. After all, if I had been told last October that ISU would field a team that would go 22-9, win the Missouri Valley Conference title, have the Player of the Year in Nate Green and the Coach of the Year in Royce Waltman, and have two other players on all-conference teams, as well as get to the NIT, I'd have taken it in a minute. I think most other fans would have taken it too.

The principle really works. I just wish I could keep it in mind when I see only the bad side of things. For instance, for every chest-thumping bonehead that I've seen preening across the screen of a televised NBA game, there's always that kid who gives it everything he has every time he's called off the bench by his high school coach to get a minute or two. For every star a coach has had, I'll bet most of them remember two kids like that. I know I do.

For every so-called die-hard fan who seems to believe that the price of admission gives him the right to abuse referees and players alike, usually by punishing the fans around him with his dimwittedness, I think there's a dozen parents who've taken their kids just to see a game and enjoy watching it together.

For every rotten game I've seen, there seems to be a classic. I watched several very good high school games at the Class A North Vermillion sectional last week, and one of the best things I can recall is that my ticket was $4, not $40.

For every ref who blows a call, stands my notion that an amazing percentage of calls are right. I watch a lot of high school basketball, and it amazes me that most of the time the referees, who also happen to be teachers or factory workers or real estate agents in their day jobs, mostly make correct calls.

One final example of my good-with-the-bad theory comes from Dale Glenn's "A History of the IHSAA." According to Glenn, it was not unusual for teams in the old days of Indiana high school basketball to breeze through their schedules without much of a challenge. Many of these schools would then look elsewhere for competition before the state tournament began.

One such team came from Amboy, a tiny burg in Miami County. The Pirates were undefeated in 1917 and proclaimed themselves 'The Small School Champions of Northern Indiana." A newspaper ad was circulated throughout the state claiming that Amboy was hopeful that a school of similar size from the southern part of the state would be interested in playing a title game. Switz City's Tigers and Coach Mark Wakefield thought themselves capable.

According to an interview with Wakefield years after the fact, his team boarded a train in Switz City, traveled to Indianapolis, boarded another train that took them to Bunker Hill—yes, we do have one in Indiana—and then took another train on to Amboy.

When his squad arrived, Wakefield was surprised to see that Amboy's gymnasium was an odd-looking wooden structure, and the playing floor was completely enveloped with chicken wire. The fans, as well as the coaches, stood outside of the cage, and since the ball merely bounced off of the chicken wire back into play, the Switz City players soon realized that in Amboy there was no such thing as being "out- of-bounds."

By the way, the Tigers overcame the grueling trip, the chicken wire, the hostile fans, and the Pirates and headed back to Greene County as the "Small School Champions of Indiana."

That's making the best of a tough situation. Let's hope the Sycamores can do the same thing today in Salt Lake City with the Longhorns.

Despite age, John Wooden remains refreshingly new
November 15, 2000

There is a story that John Wooden himself still repeats about Bill Walton.

One day the consensus all-American came to practice after a 10-day break wearing a full beard, an open violation of Wooden's policy against facial hair.

"Bill, have you forgotten something?" Wooden asked.

Walton replied that if the great coach was referring to his beard, that Wooden should understand that it was "his right" to wear it. Wooden asked his center if he "strongly" believed in that right, and Walton replied, "Yes I do. Very much."

The legendary coach then politely told his star, "Bill, I have a great respect for individuals who stand up for those things in which they believe. I really do. And the team is going to miss you."

Walton's beard was gone before the practice started.

Walton phones his old coach, now 90, nearly every day. The former UCLA and NBA legend now says, "After my father, Coach Wooden has had the most profound influence on me of anyone in my entire life."

John Wooden coached his last college basketball game 25 years ago. He was born in 1910 and raised on a farm near Martinsville. His first basketball, made by his mother, consisted of rags stuffed into a pair of sewn cotton hose. Wooden still writes love letters to a wife who died in 1985. He can recall the name of every player who ever played for him. He remains true to the adages and homilies practiced by our grandparents and their parents. And, he is thoroughly modern.

In this day and age, when many parents are regularly reading advice columns and self-help guides about raising children in this changing and challenging world, or merely throwing their hands up in frustration at the attempt, Wooden sees things as clearly as he did when his Bruins were pressing and running their way to a remarkable 10 national titles.

To many, the coach has been reduced to the dust of memories, shelved as an immortal who was great in his time, but incapable of understanding basketball and its players in a new millennium. In his day, Wooden's philosophies and rules, his anecdotes and lessons, were fine, but critics today can find little room for him in our pierced, pampered, and monied game.

But to me, Wooden remains refreshingly new. His advocation of the "Golden Rule," of teamwork and fair play, are on the cutting edge of where basketball can go. We will probably never return to the days of crewcuts, "yes sirs," and canvas hightops, but Wooden believes that basketball can and does still teach our sons and daughters the values of hard work and dedication. As he says himself, "Are people really that different today? Have times changed so much? I wonder about that."

I've told my friends and family the familiar stories: I met Wooden twice, and he is the closest thing to a hero that I have, although in his days of glory I rooted solidly against him when he brought his powerhouse teams to South Bend or Bloomington. I read his autobiography, have a framed copy of his "Pyramid of Success" on my wall. A poem the former Purdue all-American and Indiana high school English teacher wrote hangs above my office desk.

Years ago, my own players were constantly bombarded with a litany of Woodenisms: "Discipline yourself, and others won't have to;" "Big things are only accomplished through attention to minor details;" "Make sure your teammates know they are working with you, not for you." I plastered them on locker room walls, on bulletin boards, and in playbooks.

Wooden knows that there remains a difference between right and wrong, and basketball is often the teacher of that principle. Another story about Walton illustrates that.

The big redhead limped into Wooden's office one afternoon with a question about his ever-increasing knee pain. "Coach," Walton said, "I've heard that smoking marijuana will reduce the pain in my knees. Is it OK with you if I use it?"

Wooden simply answered, "Bill, I haven't heard that it is a pain reliever, but I heard that it is illegal." The discussion was over.

The legendary coach doesn't travel as far or as often as he once did and is content to live a quiet life from his cluttered Encino apartment. He has refused public comment about Bob Knight's firing, says that college basketball is losing its zeal for team play, and would like to see the dunk outlawed once again because it promotes individualism. Professional basketball holds no interest for him.

"I believe basketball is a team sport and should remain so." He says he misses the daily practices more than anything from his coaching days.

Wooden also says, that like Socrates, he "has prepared for death all his life by the life I have lived." One day we will lose him, and when we do, I'll remember the privilege of meeting him.

He is the remarkable man who has also said, "Don't let making a living prevent you from making a life."

Duties of being manager helped in preparation for life's demands December 1, 2000

Picture in your mind the typical image of a basketball team manager: brief case; pocket protector; high-water pants; maybe a little masking tape on those horn-rimmed glasses. He's always the little guy scurrying around filling water bottles and washing uniforms, tallying stats and tugging at the coach's coattail in hopes for a chance to shoot around with the guys on the team.

Then picture Craig McKee and Paul Johnson, two men who had to endure a little of that stereotyping in their high school days, but who've used their lives as basketball managers at two local high schools to springboard themselves into successful careers afterward. They were pretty important people in those days; they still are.

McKee is 42, married, and a prominent Terre Haute attorney. He graduated from Terre Haute North in 1975 and the Indiana University School of Law at Indianapolis in 1983, and, as he puts it: "To me, the connection to my days [at North] is not all that tenuous. Being a student manager started me on an interesting trail of experiences."

That trail included stints as a sportswriter in both Terre Haute and Indianapolis, a position at Indiana State as a sports information guru, and the chance to be a law clerk for Federal Judge Gene Brooks.

"Because I was never a jock by any stretch of the imagination, I concentrated on what was within my ability and never really had fantasies about being a starter on the basketball team," McKee said. "That doesn't mean

I didn't compete and win—but that was pretty much limited to table tennis. I think the managing experience gave me the best of participation in athletics—the camaraderie, friendship, sense of team—without all of the pressure that comes with being an athlete."

It was from those days, when McKee appeared as if he were 15 going on 50, that two seniors, Steve Homburg and Damon Brodhacker, started calling him "Professor." The name took.

"There are a handful of people who still call me by that name, and occasionally Carl Riddle [North's former principal] still lapses into the habit, 25 years later," McKee added.

Craig feels that his days under Howard Sharpe as a jack-of-all-trades, including his initiation of a "crude" sports information department for the Patriots, were essential in teaching him the organizational skills it takes to do what he now does for a living.

"If you carried Sharpie's keys, you knew he trusted you, and those keys could open about anything under that school's roof. Howard Sharpe expected a high degree of responsibility from student managers."

It was not without note that North's equipment room not only came with the usual assortment of basketballs and practice gear, it also came with a typewriter and desk for McKee's press guides, pre-game stats, and information sheets.

Johnson is 25, single, and currently works for Ford Credit in Irving, Texas. He graduated from Riverton Parke in 1993, and like McKee, attended Indiana State for his undergraduate degrees; his are in Business Administration and Quality and Decision Systems. Affectionately called "PJ" during his years as a manager,

Johnson served as the "Voice of the Panthers"—the public address announcer at home games—for over five years. He managed an incredible 11 boys and girls basketball teams in the years from his 7th to 12th grades. In that time, he kept scorebooks, did laundry, set up the gym—a three-and-a-half hour task—for all home games, greeted visiting teams, and helped coordinate the biddy basketball programs at two elementary schools.

"I was usually the first one to arrive at the school on Saturday morning at 6 or 6:30... It was great to see the excitement in the kids and parents, but after a full a-day of school on Friday, and an away game on Friday night, returning home at midnight or sometimes later, it was tough to be back at school that early the next morning," Johnson says.

Johnson also knows that his job as a manager helped him tackle the task of leading ten other Ford employees in their jobs everyday.

"Organization was an important lesson that I learned. I look back now and see that a teenager was given a lot of responsibility... You have to be organized, have great use of time management, be able to think a problem through from start to finish, before you start doing something about it. It was tough to gain respect from people who thought someone else was better suited for the job I was doing, but when that respect was earned, it was a wonderful feeling."

Despite owning a bundle of fond memories of his days at Riverton, Johnson did relate three of his best. "One of the funniest things that happened to me was being locked in the girls' locker room after returning from a late night road trip. You have to understand that Riverton's locker rooms are underground—no windows.

Luckily I was able to get a coach's attention before he left. Most guys might want to be in the girls' locker room, but I'm glad I didn't have to spent the night there."

Johnson also recalled the night an irate coach flung off his jacket, only to smack Paul across the face with a fully loaded key ring. "From that game forward for the next three years, every time he started to take off his coat, I would jump up and slide it off for him. I don't think he got his frustration release, but I never got hit with any more keys either."

In 1993, Johnson not only received the largest plaque at the school's sports banquet, he was honored with the Marion Crawley Memorial Scholarship from the Indiana Basketball Coaches Association.

Finally, McKee joked that he was "patiently waiting" for the folks at the Indiana Basketball Hall of Fame in New Castle to open its "Legendary Managers Wing."

If they ever do, I'll have two names for them.

You don't have to go far to find something special
February 28, 2001

If you own a computer, there's a good chance that lately you've had an e-mail list forwarded to you called, "You Know You're a Hoosier If..."

Despite it being a bit bluenosed, I have to admit that most of the entries on the thing ring true. As No. 12 suggests, I must be a dyed-in-the-wool Hoosier because I have stacked hay, taken a dip in a pond to clean off, and still had the strength left over to "play a couple of games of hoops all in the same day."

Yes, I do know several people who have hit a deer (No. 1); I do, indeed, drink "pop" (No. 17); and, it is true that I know a few folks who have large belt buckles with their initials on them (No. 59).

While there are a number of people out there who consider most Hoosiers little more than country bumpkins and hayseeds, the 23rd item on that list caught my attention and made me reconsider just how lucky I am to live where I do. It reads: "A high school basketball game draws a bigger crowd on the weekend nights than movie theaters." That must not be true in other places.

Each year I'm amazed by the number of people who come to my county to look at covered bridges and fall foliage, but I know what brings them here, and it's the reason I've never left. It seems that it often takes visitors to help me see just how special my home place truly is.

Bill Gildea is such a visitor. Gildea wrote the highly successful book, "Where the Game Matters Most" in 1998, and this Washington Post writer seems to be a kindred spirit. He too thinks Indiana basketball—both the college and high school varieties—is a pretty special thing living in a special place. He told me so when we spoke at a local bookshop a few years ago.

In a recent column in the Post, Gildea wrote of the listless, "emotionless" attitude of the fans at an NBA game he'd watched in Philadelphia, but that "no one took matter-of-factly the three games [he] witnessed in the heartland" later that week.

Where had Gildea seen those games? First, he traveled to Anderson's Wigwam, the world's second largest high school gymnasium, to watch the hometown

Indians take on New Castle in a typical Friday night winter scrap.

He poetically described how most of the 2,000 New Castle fans came to arrive in Anderson: "The caravan is a common sight in Indiana; when the town team is 15-1, the ritual lines of headlights winding through the farmland can be extraordinarily long."

The next afternoon Gildea was at Hulman Center in Terre Haute watching what he called a "scantily reported epic" between Indiana State and Missouri Valley Conference rival Illinois State. An unabashed admirer of ISU's Michael Menser, Gildea said of the Sycamore's star guard, "Menser is the kind of player that opposing coaches seek out to congratulate after a game."

Later that evening, Gildea took two of his companions east to Indianapolis to see Hinkle Fieldhouse. All but one door to the place was locked when they got to the Butler campus, but as he put it, "What we did, three adults, was sit in the first row in virtual darkness and marvel at this 15,000-seat temple thinking of historic high school and college games played there, looking at— if anything is perfect—the perfect basketball floor."

On Sunday, Gildea and his buddies headed to Bloomington to watch the Hoosiers play Michigan. Despite a poorly played game, he wrote, "But Assembly Hall is a theater devoted to basketball. Five red NCAA championship banners hang at one end. Basketball coaches at various levels attended; the sport was the talk."

Perhaps the one experience from Gildea's journeys to Indiana that best describes what he must feel about our state was related in an interview that he gave three years ago. Gildea has always been interested in the state's favorite sons, and a few miles outside of

Fairmount he found the barn in which actor James Dean honed his childhood basketball skills.

When the writer asked a Fairmount acquaintance, who just happened to have been a pallbearer for Dean, to call the barn's owner to seek permission for the writer to look around, he was amazed at the response. The farmer said, "Just send him over; I won't be here, but tell him to drive in and just raise the latch on the barn and slide the door to the right. Only have one rule: Don't smoke in the barn and close the door on the way out."

As the writer said, "That's the kind of generosity that I found there."

So, in reference to that e-mail list again, perhaps I do carry jumper cables in my car regularly (No. 16), or I can see "at least two basketball hoops from my yard (No. 27)." And, it is true, "Technically, I don't even live in a town (No. 52)."

And I don't think I'd have it any other way.

Basketball officials may have greatest love of the game
March 28, 2001

Despite being a rather talkative guy, Steve Morris hopes that nobody notices him much. That is, when he's doing his night job.

Morris is a basketball official, and has been for quite a while now. He's worked at nearly every school in the Wabash Valley: junior high, varsity or junior-varsity, girls or boys. The fact is, Morris is really like the average referee I've known. He wants to do his job well and go unnoticed while doing it.

I've heard it before. Why would anybody in their right mind want to be a referee? It's a question more and more people are asking and soon the competent basketball official may be a pretty rare breed.

"A good official is an individual who has a love of the game, has the ability to communicate with all types of players and coaches, and has to be one who can handle stressful situations without getting nervous," Morris says diplomatically. "He has to know the rules and he has to be someone who is always striving to improve. I'll only be satisfied with doing a better job in the next game that I work," he adds.

Morris takes great pride in being called a "typical ref" too. Like so many others, he got his start as a volunteer, was inspired by two experienced officials to get better, and now takes pleasure in playing a big part in basketball games.

"I first got into officiating basketball when the church league that my brother and I were playing in needed officials. We gave it a shot, and then after a few games, I was hooked. I started working junior high and men's rec leagues to get experience and then moved up to the junior-varsity and varsity level games," Morris said.

A Terre Haute North grad, Morris has been married for nearly 25 years. He's worked for Ardico for 23 of those as an area restaurant supervisor and spends what little free time he has proudly keeping up on the exploits of his two children, Travis and Megan. And, of course, even when he was still asking patrons if they wanted fries with their orders, he found the time to officiate.

"I admired two excellent local officials, Dean Russell and Joe Reed, and I wanted to emulate them,"

Morris said. "They were [are] very good, and they seemed to be having a great time officiating."

To be honest, I've often wondered about the near-masochistic attraction that people like Steve have to being a referee. I've always been at a loss to explain why anyone would want to hustle out of work, cram down a hasty supper, and face the Hoosier roads in the winter, only to spend a few hours enduring a pressure cooker of insults, venomous fans, and potential embarrassment. But then again, I don't look at things the way Steve Morris does.

"What I enjoy most is being involved with the student-athletes, the kids, on a regular basis and getting to experience the thrill of competition with them. I also enjoy being a part of a group of individuals who have the same interests as I do. It's actually like a big fraternity and a family atmosphere among officials. Most of my closest friends are the people I officiate with," Morris says.

"My motivation, first and foremost, is to have fun while officiating and to continue to improve my on-court abilities and experiences. I also want to move up the ladder with the ultimate goal of working the state finals in girls or boys basketball. I'm also motivated by the extremely talented group of people whom I officiate with on a regular basis and the high standards that they set."

There's something that Morris does dislike about his nights trying to get every call correct, and he's diplomatic about that too.

"What I enjoy least of all are fans that, shall I say, have a limited grasp of the rules of the game and how it should be officiated. They think officials are out to get them and their team. You know, we really don't care who wins," he noted.

Morris's respect for his profession is obvious, especially when he lists the games he's most enjoyed. Among those was working his first boys sectional in the last year of non-class basketball; getting to work a girls regional this past season with regular partner and good friend, Greg Hayes; working at New Castle in the Hall of Fame Classic this year; and calling a Special Olympics game in historic Hinkle Fieldhouse.

"I know this will sound corny, but just having the opportunity to officiate basketball in the best state in the country is the real highlight for me," Morris says. "My officiating philosophy is to have fun, get it right, and represent myself and my association at a high level at all times."

As I've said, you have to be a little crazy to want to be a referee. Or, to love being one as much as Steve Morris does.

Scoring 100 points just isn't what it used to be
February 14, 2001

There are basketball fans who think that what Cedrick Hensley and Dajuan Wagner have accomplished is something wonderful; there are others who think what they've done a disgrace.

In case you haven't heard about it, Hensley scored 101 points in a 178-28 win for Heritage Christian Academy in Cleveland, Texas, late last month. On that same night, Wagner, who is headed for the University of

Memphis next fall, racked up an even 100 as his team in Camden, N.J., won 157-67.

With their feats, Hensley and Wagner became only the 13th and 14th high school players in history to hit triple digits in a single game, and some folks are calling their prolific scoring remarkable. They think that 100-point games are such a rarity that it's time to break out the party hats.

Others are in favor of Hensley's and Wagner's coaches getting a little tar and a few feathers for their apparent lack of class in leaving their star players in such lopsided games. To them, these players are no less than the latest signposts that we live in an age of excess. I have to admit that watching a kid score 100 points in a game decided by 90 or more is a little like unwrapping underwear on Christmas morning.

In Wagner's case, it's already a given that he's headed for a Division I program and needs no name recognition. As for Hensley, the word is that he was scheduled for minor surgery and his coach, Jerome Tang, wanted to play the 6-foot-4 star the entire game since he'll be out of the line-up for a few weeks. Besides, Tang supposedly asked his opponent, Banff Christian's Geoff Norton, if he was "OK" with leaving Hensley in the game. What a guy.

You might be surprised to know that the only player in the annals of Indiana high school basketball to break the 100-point mark was Herman "Suz" Sayger of Culver High School. He did it, believe it or not, on March 8, 1913, and unlike Hensley and Wagner, had no 3-point shot available to him.

Sayger poured in 113 points against Winamac, a school that fielded a team for the first time that season.

Sayger's Indians apparently showed no mercy either as Culver won 154-10 with Suz connecting on 56 field goals and one free throw. Sayger also scored 76 in another game that year.

Still think that high scoring in the old days was a fluke? The second highest point total in the Indiana record books was set even earlier. On December 11, 1908, Guy Barr of Rochester pumped in 97 points, and his team whipped Bremen 139-9. Barr hit 47 field goals and three free throws that day in Rochester's Armory Hall.

There's a reasonably local connection to the third highest scoring total, and it's an old one too. In 1917, Snowden Hert of Newberry scored 90 points as the River Rats crushed Worthington 140-2 in what obviously wasn't a friendly backyard rivalry.

For me, the most compelling story about high scoring games was that of Danny Heater of Burnsville, WV. For over 40 years Heater has owned the single game scoring mark with an incredible 135-point game on January 26, 1960. In an interview carried last year by the Associated Press, Heater simply said of the game, "I was happy and sad at the same time. I was embarrassed. I wasn't raised that way to embarrass people. I didn't know what to say."

Heater's coach, Jack Stalnaker, later claimed that he regretted allowing Heater to score so much in the 173-43 win over Widen High, but he did have a motive. Heater's father was dying of lung cancer, and despite the boy's scoring average of 27 points a game, the 6-1 guard wasn't being recruited by colleges. Stalnaker wanted Heater to break the state scoring mark of 74 points; perhaps it would help a good kid from a poor family.

By halftime Heater had 50, and Burnsville owned a 75-17 lead. Early in the second half Stalnaker called a timeout to take his star out of the game just after Heater had broken the state mark. But most of the Burnsville players expressed an interest in Heater staying in to perhaps set a national record. Stalnaker gave in, and Heater scored 55 more points in the game's final 10 minutes.

Heater's numbers that night made a season for other players: 53-of-70 from the field and 29-of-40 from the free throw line. He also had 32 rebounds and seven assists.

Ironically, Heater never received a scholarship offer. Despite a donation that paid for his college tuition at Richmond, he soon left campus for Burnsville, homesick and guilty over leaving his family.

For the boy who had the greatest scoring night in history, there apparently were things in his life more important than basketball.

Third Quarter
Fall 2001-Winter 2008

Sometimes you don't know what you've got 'til it's gone... October 26, 2000

You don't have to be a wizard to figure out that when those airliners crashed into the World Trade Center towers and the Pentagon last month that the world changed. As we've been reminded numerous times: things will never be the same.

Anthrax and smart bombs, the Taliban and "ground zero" have moved to the forefront of our thinking, and worrying about bio-terrorism seems to have neatly replaced our concerns about that leaking water heater in the basement or next month's house payment.

Yet, it's October now, and even though we can't push the horrors that Osama bin Laden has handed to us out of our minds, I'm reminded by the falling leaves and autumn's cold rains that change, often the bad variety, is always a part of our lives. I'm not sure that we've ever collectively experienced the uncertainties of this past month before, but in times of even mild anxiety, I always seem to try to grab onto something familiar, something sound.

One of those security blankets of mine gets unrolled this week in most gymnasiums around the state. High school basketball is one of those traditions that marks the calendars of our lives, takes us back to safer, more simple times, when all we had to do to make our mark was toss a leather ball through an iron hoop or cram into the bleachers to watch the biggest game of the year. No, the arguments of returning to single-class tournament, or whether it's a zone or a man-to-man defense for our favorite teams, aren't going to compare with the importance of strategic missile strikes on Al-Qaida bases or the growing menace of evil coming to our houses with a 34-cent stamp attached. But, we're going to the gymnasiums this winter to watch basketball games, and very little, save the blast of an Arctic snowstorm and slick country roads, will stop us.

For me, it's back this week to coaching junior high basketball, and hopefully my battery is recharged and ready for the long haul of late-night bus rides, undigested suppers, and the special gut-churning anxiety that only a coach knows much about.

Somewhere along the line, with my coaching and teaching lives running full-bore, I have a column to write, and in tough times with it, as well, I also head back to what's familiar and comforting. I believe we have something special in the Wabash Valley: we're rich in both basketball folklore and basketball folks, and I get paid to write about them.

I know I'm taking the long way "round the barn" here, but basketball is one of those simple things that enables us to securely hold onto something while the world around us seems to pass up crazy on the way to frightening.

In the long run, it won't be critically important to national defense or homeland security if our favorite number two guard can improve his left hand before the sectional tournament begins; whether our home team can win conference games on the road or not; even if the coach can or can't teach the zone press. But, it does matter.

There's a certainty, a safe harbor for me, when I see generations of basketball families sitting in the bleachers together, or when I wander down darkened hallways looking through the dusty glass of display cases that hold the images of yesterday's heroes. I grin when I take my son to the barbershop, and in mid-crew cut, it's basketball that crops up as the topic of conversation, often among total strangers.

This year in particular, basketball will help take our minds off of what we know is not going to go away anytime soon. If what our President is telling us to do is right—to get on with our everyday lives—then let's get on with them this fall on Friday and Saturday nights at the gym.

I can't think of two people who differ more than the real Joni Mitchell and the fictional Myra Fleener, but in light of recent events, what they've said still rings true in my ears. Mitchell is still belting out folksy blues tunes, just like she did over 30 years ago at the height of the Vietnam War. On the other hand, Fleener alternately scolded, defended, and loved Coach Norman Dale in Hoosiers, the Holy Grail of basketball movies.

In her song, "Big Yellow Taxi," Mitchell repeats the refrain, "Don't it always seem to go, that you don't know what you've got 'til it's gone." And, it was Fleener who tells Dale that when she was away from the tiny town of Hickory for a few years, "... there were a few things I missed not being here. I missed knowing that nothing ever changes; people never change. It makes you feel real solid."

I can't argue with them at all. I believe that too.

No one can really fill the vacant chair
November 7, 2001

I'm not sure what Bernard Gideon would think if he could know that an old Civil War song reminds me of him, but I think he'd at least grin a little. Bernard passed away this summer, and I'll miss him most this winter. He was a teacher and a friend of mine for over 20 years, and I don't think anyone taught me as much about basketball as he did.

I think he taught me a few other things too.

Chances are that if you remember seeing Bernard in recent years, you caught a glimpse of him sitting in a stiff plastic cafeteria chair near the railing on the landing at one end of Riverton Parke's gymnasium. Bernard had been betrayed by his weak heart for years, and he couldn't travel very far or very often from his house unless it was for something truly important like a basketball game.

I was a member of the cadre of former coaching buddies and friends who would rub elbows with Bernard at those games. We'd gossip a little bit about the latest basketball news and second-guess coaches' decisions and referees' calls even more.

He always insisted on buying a round of popcorn and drinks for us, but he gave away more than that. He may have forgotten a name from one week to the next, occasionally had trouble seeing the scoreboard too, but I don't think Bernard ever really forgot much about basketball, or ever lost his respect for the game either. Bernard simply loved basketball. It didn't matter whether it was fifth graders, junior high girls, or a pick-up game on the concrete court near his house, he'd watch.

By the time I first got into coaching years ago, Bernard had given it up for the last time. He was content to teach grade school physical education and was the athletic director at Montezuma High School. I'd often stop by his desk in the afternoons—he never had an office to himself—and pick his brain for a drill or a play or a piece of advice. I think it was the advice I came to cherish the most.

I remember that he thought I got too "excited" when I coached. He told me that my temper made my job all the more difficult when I was both enraged at a poor call and yet still had to coolly lead my team. I'm positive that in Bernard's early coaching years he too was a bit high-spirited, but I also know that a former assistant of his told me that Bernard could often be overheard humming hymns while his team performed on the floor.

Bernard came from humble beginnings, worked hard to earn a living, and taught and coached his entire career at small schools in small towns. He learned to be satisfied and happy with simple things, his friends and family, and sometimes with moral victories when a lack of talent or size meant real ones were impossible.

The first time I met him, Bernard was still coaching. His tiny underdog Aztecs were to be first-round sectional fodder for the host Patriots at Terre Haute North, a school roughly 15 times the size of Montezuma. Gideon's squad lost by 30, but at times his team gave its bigger opponents fits, and the Aztecs did it with a 6-1 center and three other starters under 5-8.

I was supposed to be impartial, but I didn't want Bernard's team to lose that night. Even North's Howard Sharpe told me after the game, "He [Gideon] got everything his kids had to give."

Now, why did that old song remind me of Bernard? When the unexpected slaughter of the War Between the States became more apparent by the fall of 1861, Henry Washburn wrote a song that eventually became a battlefield standard. It was called "The Vacant Chair." As far as I know, Bernard never hummed that tune; probably never heard it. But it applies to him. The opening line goes, "We shall meet, but we shall miss him. There will be one vacant chair..."

This winter, when his friends meet by the railing to watch a game, we'll know that no one can really fill Bernard's chair. But if I knew anything at all about Coach Gideon, I'd say he'd want someone to sit in it anyway. After all, they might miss a good game.

Some things are worth repeating
November 21, 2001

"There are only two plays: 'Romeo and Juliet' and put the darn ball in the hole." — Abe Lemons

If it's true that poor writers have to resort to using quotations when they have no original thoughts of their own, I stand guilty as charged. But, contrary to what my elementary school teachers claimed, I do listen to what other people have to say. To think I wasted all of that valuable class time standing in the hallway...

As a coach who sought a little secondhand inspiration for his team, I used to post quotes in my locker room or printed them on handouts for my players whenever I could. I don't think I know a coach who hasn't tried to stir up a little extra excitement for his players by dropping a line or two from a big-time coach or player.

For instance, in an effort to get my kids to think a bit better, I used a line from Bob Knight, who once said in reference to basketball, "Mental is to physical as four is to one. It says the truth about the game." Knight may not be very popular with the faculty at Texas Tech, but surely the Math Department is happy with that statement.

Another of my favorites came from John Wooden. It was the Wizard of Westwood who said, "The only place that success is before work is in the dictionary." Work is just as tough to sell to players now, but I'd give them a double dose of Wooden: "Success is never final, and failure is never fatal. It's courage that counts."

I truly miss Al McGuire. The former Marquette coach was refreshingly honest in a profession well stocked with phonies. McGuire once said that, "Winning is overemphasized. The only time it is really important is in surgery and war." There are a number of coaches who should write that one down.

Now, who says coaches aren't concerned with their players' academic lives? That wasn't the case at Texas A&M when Coach Shelby Metcalf discovered that one of his recruits had four Fs and a D in his first semester. "Son, it looks to me like you're spending too much time on one subject," Metcalf said.

Talking about a coach trying to get through to a player reminds me of Frank Layden of the Utah Jazz. Layden once asked a player, "Son, what is it with you? Is it ignorance or apathy?" The player replied, "Coach, I don't know, and I don't care." It's hard to argue with that logic.

Speaking of players, a senior on the University of Pittsburgh basketball squad reportedly said, "I'm going to graduate on time, no matter how long it takes." He must have been a history major.

Any coach can tell you that basketball can be a culturally enlightening experience for players. For example, Lakers' center Shaquille O'Neal was asked if he'd visited the Parthenon on his trip to Greece. The big man said, "I can't really remember the names of the clubs we went to." He shouldn't be disappointed; I don't think Patrick Ewing went there either.

You can't be lacking in intelligence to play the game. Ask Vlade Divac, the Sacramento Kings center. Divac once explained his theory on why we gain weight as we age. "We all get heavier as we get older because there's a lot more information in our heads." With that idea in mind, I'm considering tossing out all of my books so I can eat more.

Don't let anybody say that Michael Jordan will be the only reason the Washington Wizards become winners. After all, it was Wizards' Coach Doug Collins, who as a television commentator several years ago, said, "Any time Detroit scores more than 100 points and holds the other team below 100 points, they almost always win." That's breaking things down in simple enough terms.

In the long run though, I still like the old-fashioned, inspirational quote, the kind that commands center attention on locker doors and playbook covers. Allen Iverson won't have much room on my bulletin board this winter despite his talent, but Grant Hill might. The Orlando star once said, "I grew up to always respect authority, and I respect those in charge."

Better yet are Jordan's words. He said, "Even when I'm old and gray, I won't be able to play it, but I'll still love the game."

I sure wish I'd said that.

Remembering Christmas, Colts, and Captain Colliflower
December 19, 2001

When I was a kid, it seemed as though the first package I opened on most Christmas mornings was a dud. It may have had the glitziest paper, may have had just enough shape to pique my interest, but invariably it would be underwear or socks or a belt.

I thought there should have been a law against such things being considered gifts, and at one time I thought of seceding from my family—that is, until I spoke with a few other kids who experienced the same thing.

Well, now I'm older. Instead of eagerly awaiting Santa, I'm desperately trying to avoid looking like him. I still anticipate opening gifts, and I honestly think that this year one of my favorite presents may come a day late: The Pizza Hut Wabash Valley Classic gets underway the day after Christmas.

There may still be a few office parties and leftover eggnog around; the plastic reindeer may still be lit, and the after-Christmas sales may have a full head of steam, but I want to see good high school basketball, and the Classic a season ago delivered like any worthy St. Nicholas.

Perhaps the best, and most weighty, thing about the Classic is the long tradition that this new version has packed on its shoulders, Much of what made the old tournament what it was remains an integral part of the new one: it's inexpensive, colorful, and crowded.

I don't, however, see a time when the Classic can go back to the days of the school-day, 16-team finals. Schools used to let out and bused their students down to Seventh and Chestnut streets to watch their teams play in the old Indiana State gymnasium in those days. Most had used their county tournaments as their "prelims" to get there.

It's true, times were different in the heyday of the old Valley, and nothing proves that better than the scorecard from the 1933 tournament I came across a few days ago. It measures only 6 by 8 inches, and despite being folded into quarters, it listed the entire rosters of all 16 finalists. They included the Clay City Eels, the Tangier Tigers, the Perrysville Eagles, the Linton Miners, Bruceville's Hilltoppers, and Pleasantville's Blue Streaks.

The tournament that year was won by Hutsonville, Ill. The Tigers slapped Terre Haute Wiley around 35-18 in the semifinal and earned the right to face the Rosedale Colts (they wouldn't be Hotshots for a few more years), who had taken out Bainbridge 21-20. The Pointers had used just five players in that loss. Hutsonville was led that year by its team captain, center Dolph Colliflower, who scored 15 points against the Red Streaks (pretty impressive numbers in those days).

As Allen Dibble reported in the Terre Haute Tribune the morning after the championship game with Rosedale, the Tigers had a hero on their hands.

"Captain Colliflower, easily the outstanding star of the tournament, scored 17 points during the contest, falling only one point shy of the total of the entire Rosedale team." The Colts fell 29-18.

Dibble's story also gave me a glimpse of what the old Valley's games were like, and what the new Classic can become. In often excruciating detail, he wrote a minute-by-minute account of the game, and included more than one telling paragraph.

"Coach 'Red' Garrigus shifted the Rosedale lineup for the title tiff, starting Newton and Huffman at forwards, Adams at center, McCurdy and Bostick at guards... Enthusiasm swept through the crowd as the teams gathered for the final huddle, and Referee 'Chick' Springer announced that the Tribune-Star Trophy (a large silver basketball) would be given to the winner. When the trophy was flashed, the crowd yelled like mad."

This new tournament won't replace the old one; it wasn't meant to. It will simply have to carve out its own identity, and if we're as receptive to the idea behind the Classic now as folks were years ago when Captain Colliflower dominated the key, this tourney will do just fine.

Perhaps I'll see you on the 26th at the gym. I'll be the one wearing a brand new belt; I asked for one this year.

Murray Melton: A real All-American
January 16, 2002

I spoke with a hero on the phone last weekend; got a letter in the mail from him a week ago. The thing is, he doesn't think he's anything special: just a basketball fan. For some guys, honesty, devotion, and playing by the rules just come naturally, I guess.

Murray Melton of Marshall, Ill., remembers the way basketball used to be. I take it that he's the kind of guy who's not going to gripe about a few rocks in his shoes along life's roadway either. He'd read a column of mine that brought back a few memories, and he wanted to tell me about them.

I called Melton not long after I opened his letter; I had to tell him that his reminiscences truly meant something to me. They took me back a ways too; maybe even all the way to Hutsonville in the early 40s, where it's really impossible for me to go, even in memory.

Melton is 76 years old and a retired state trooper. He spent some time in the Navy during World War II, as did his two brothers. His father died when he was just a sophomore in high school, leaving seven kids at home for his mother to raise. His basketball days go all the way back to a tiny two-room schoolhouse at West York, where in the fall of the year he and his buddies dragged hoes to school just so they could scrape the grass off their outside court for basketball games. After all, they wanted the ball to "bounce somewhat true:' That story even impresses Melton's great-grandson, Boo Davis.

Murray remembers that after the regular season was over, all of the county teams traveled to Robinson to play a tournament. "Teams with names like Draper, Ball, Star, Montgomery, South Union, and many others I don't recall, were there," he says. But one team that he could never forget—Grassy Hollow—was there too, and it was an all-girl squad.

"They all had fingernails about a half-inch or more long," Melton said. "They didn't care whether they got the ball or not, as long as they left a red scratch somewhere. That bothered some of the team, but I grew up with four sisters (just normal)," he wrote in that letter. Melton mentioned that his team had two girls on it as well, but they didn't get to play much. "They had to wear those bloomers, you know."

From West York, Murray went on to play high school ball at Hutsonville. "We sure didn't lose any games from being out of shape...after practice five of us trotted home, three to West York (five miles) and two on to West Union (three more miles). There were very few vehicles on the road then because of the war and gas ration[ing]. We sure were dedicated, huh?"

Melton remembers the friends he had at Hutsonville, the great coach he had in "Ped" Huffman, the tough competition he faced, and the glory days of the Wabash Valley Tourney.

"Our coach always gave the team Hutsonville's allotted tickets. Five, I think. I always wanted to go [to the Valley] on the first day so I could see all sixteen teams play. We would leave home before sun-up, and, of course, get home after midnight. What a great day."

Memories from the 1943 Valley—won by Brazil—stood out in Melton's memory. He recalled that Joe Short (who played on the 1940 Valley champion Flat Rock team) and two other friends who attended Indiana State with him, stood on the floor of the ISU gymnasium and tossed fudgesicles up to the back rows, then caught coins in return, rarely missing the thrown money.

Why didn't Melton's Tigers ever make it to the final rounds of the tournament in Terre Haute? "We had a pretty good team, but when you play teams like Flat Rock (champs in '40), Palestine (champs in '41), and Paris (state champ in '43 and runner-up in '42), you accumulated a lot of losses from some very good teams."

By the way, Melton will soon be married 56 years to the Flat Rock cheerleader he met in 1943 when he played a game on the Wildcats' home floor. "There was a friend of ours who went with us to the ballgames, and he'd get addresses of girls for us. During the JV game, we'd sometimes go and sit in the other school's crowd just to get them excited. So anyway, I remember her (wife, Norma) saying to me, 'Get your feet off my seat.' Well, I got her address," Melton said.

In his letter, Melton called his wife "a real doll," and Norma at 76, despite health problems, must still be. Her husband mentioned at least three times in our phone conversation that "she really is beautiful."

These days, Melton still watches a lot of basketball with his friends. They'll drive to Evansville or New Castle if they want to. For instance, he recently took in Marshall's games at the Pizza Hut Wabash Valley Classic at Terre Haute North. "I have to just sit and read about what I used to be able to do," he says with a husky laugh.

Melton has a boatload of basketball memories. Ask him how he played games in a converted LST during his time in the South Pacific, or why Hutsonville's gym was supposed to have more bleachers, or about the coal stoves and chimneys he learned to avoid while playing in gyms on the road. But those are "a whole 'nother story," he'll say.

To close his letter, Melton wrote, "Yours in Memories." Murray, I think you worded that perfectly.

Cold weather just another excuse to talk basketball
February 27, 2002

In search of a pack of gum just a few balmy days ago, I stood in a convenience store checkout line behind a woman wearing cutoffs and sandals. Since it's a scientific fact that basketball and Bermuda shorts are opposing forces in nature, and that going without socks in mid-February always precipitates a blast of Arctic air, this week's cold weather moved me to consider an oft-asked question: What's the best basketball game I've ever watched?

Besides taking a while to mull over an answer myself, I posed that rocking-chair topic to a pair of friends, Larry Adamson and Mike Carty. Their opinions always interest me, whether they come via e-mail from hundreds of miles away, as Larry's do, or from Mike as he walks on the treadmill next to mine during an early-morning workout.

Adamson graduated from Pimento High School in 1960, in fact attended all 12 grades in that small community, and earned bachelor's and master's degrees in education from Indiana State in 1967. He taught and coached at Rockville and Frankfort High Schools, eventually moved to Nashville, Tenn. for a while, and since the late 1970s has been working for the U.S. Golf Association as its director of championship administration for the last 23 years.

As Larry put it, "It's hard for an old Hoosier to think he lives just 45 miles west of the Lincoln Tunnel, the Empire State Building and New York City. That's a long way from the Pimentos, Prairie Creeks, Blackhawks and Rileys of Indiana."

Larry says my question was a tough one for any Hoosier, but he had no trouble in supplying plenty of answers for me. "I guess one game I would mention would have to be one I saw in the mid-'60s in the Indiana state high school tournament, the regional, that [took place] in Frankfort. At that time, I believe it was my first year of teaching and coaching at Frankfort. The game was between Speedway, out of Indianapolis, and Bainbridge. Now, Bainbridge was a very small school, but it had a great reputation for basketball. Pat Rady was coaching Bainbridge, and Morris Pollard was the coach at Speedway," Adamson recalled.

"I believe Bainbridge ended up winning that game, but it was one that when it was over, you wanted to go into both lockerrooms, hug every kid, and tell them what a great job they did in representing themselves, their school, and community."

Adamson was particularly awed by the Pointers' Larry Steele, who played "... in the mold of Larry Bird. I can't remember the score, but it was a game that was just back and forth, and it was played so well. I also remember sitting just a few seats away from Joe B. Hall, at that time the coach at Kentucky. I talked with him during and after that game, and, of course, Steele was recruited by and did go to Kentucky. One of the things that I remember Hall saying was how great of a game it had been. Frankfort's gym held about 5,000, and it was rocking and full."

Carty graduated from Clinton High School in 1969 and now serves as the chief financial officer of First Financial Corporation in Terre Haute. His favorite game came, not while he helped his team get to the final round of the regional at Bloomington in 1968 (they lost in two overtimes), but in the season before as he sat in the bleachers of the old Clinton gymnasium after playing in a junior-varsity contest. It was early February 1967.

"I had just finished playing in the B-game against Garfield. There was truly a level of animosity between the teams. I can't really remember why, I just know that the gym was highly charged... I remember the noise that was generated in that old gym," he said.

"After we showered, we came upstairs to watch the varsity game. Clinton was having a good year and had beaten six of the Vigo County schools to that point, including a buzzer-beater against Gerstmeyer a week or so earlier."

Garfield was led that year by two all-state candidates at guard: Howard Williams and Mike Turner, and the Purple Eagles' big man, Paul Siebenmorgan, would go on to play at ISU. The Wildcats had only two seniors, the Bentons [Ray and Marty], while their leading scorer was junior Jim Virostko.

Carty added, "Garfield was 18-2 that year and ranked in the state. They had tremendous fan support, as did Clinton. Those of us who had the opportunity to play in that old gym can still remember the great acoustics there. On that night, the place was so loud you couldn't hear yourself talk. That's when I realized what Hoosier Hysteria was all about. The electricity generated for that game by the fans was amazing."

It was ironic, but like Adamson, Carty used the same vivid verb to describe the environment for his favorite game.

"Although Garfield showed everyone why they deserved the state ranking, it was a game I will remember, not for the play, but for the great fans," Carty said. "When a high school team puts forth the effort to excel, the community rallies around them and those gyms really rocked."

Oh, my choice for the greatest game? I put together a list of favorites, but I don't think I've seen one better than Terre Haute South's 79-77 double-overtime win over Van Buren in Hulman Center in the second game of the regional in March 1978, but talking about that one will have to wait for another snap of cold weather.

In closing a recent note to me, Adamson said something else I had to share.

"Often, I think back to the 1950s and basketball, and I think about what it did for me. That might sound confusing to some folks because I wasn't a particularly good player. I went to a small high school and didn't go on to any type of greatness. But I think of the attitudes, the work ethic, and all the various things that were instilled in me by those teachers and coaches through basketball... I believe there are countless others out of that time who have the same story. I guess that's what made Indiana high school basketball special. I'm grateful," Larry said.

Hopefully, there's a new generation of players out there who will be able to say the very same thing some day.

Another year gone, but good memories keep coming back
April 26, 2002

There's an old joke about a man who buys a lamp at a garage sale, then discovers that its magical. A genie emerges from the lamp and tells him that he can receive one of three things: money, love, or great wisdom. The man eagerly chooses the wisdom. The genie grants it to him, then asks the man if he has any regrets about his decision.

"I should have taken the money," the guy says.

I've had a few regrets this year, but writing Sidelines isn't one of then. It may be a bit cool this week, but it's clearly springtime now, and basketball season is over, so this column is closing up shop for the summer, as well. I'll stash a few story ideas in my mind's messy filing cabinets for a few months, then pull them out when the leaves begin to fall in October.

In the past, I've always ended the writing season with a story, and this year is no exception. I don't think I've ever underappreciated the fact that as a coach I've had the privilege of getting to know hundreds of kids. Most stay on my team in memory.

One of those special kids was Lisa Persinger Thomas. Lisa never played varsity ball for me, but years ago, as a junior-varsity player at Montezuma, she was on our team for what I now know is the only real reason to play basketball: to enjoy it.

Lisa passed away last summer, and what was so shocking about her death was that she was one of the most energetic people I've ever known. She didn't have an off switch. Lisa couldn't slow down; not on the basketball floor, not in life. She was 5-feet-nothing, but she had a great big heart. I guess it just gave out on her.

In the winter of 1983, my team was getting ready for a road game to a neighboring county. My junior-varsity coach, Jim Harper, called to tell me that because of a conflict at work, I'd have to coach both games that night. I'll never forget what happened.

Lisa, and another wonderful kid, Annie Branson (now a teacher herself), were our starting guards that night, and despite the fact that they had struggled all season in a few key areas—like passing, dribbling, and shooting—we found our team up 20-0 at the half.

When that lead grew to 30-0 after the third quarter, every girl on the team agreed that we had to allow the other team to score. As I said, I had a group of good kids. They wanted to win, but they also knew what it felt like to lose. We wanted to let the other team get good shots, and Lisa and Annie had to help them.

We stood in place so our opponents could drive around us; we allowed rebounds to drop; we even intentionally fouled players to get them to the free throw line. With about three minutes left in the game, I called a timeout to diagram a way we could help them even more.

After a turnover gave us the ball back, I told Lisa to dribble toward her defensive man, pass her the ball, then just step out of the way. Lisa dribbled up the floor and promptly passed the ball off her opponent's foot. It rolled out of bounds, and we kept possession.

Annie inbounded the ball to Lisa again, who then spent a little time frenetically dribbling around in what strangely resembled one of those Globetrotter gags where the Washington Generals pretend to play defense. I screamed, "Lisa, pass the ball now!"

She did. The pass hit the player guarding her square in the face. After the officials helped the young lady off the floor, it was our ball, again...

To their credit, Lisa and Annie and their teammates never stopped trying to help their opponents score. They never did.

But, when I think of those kids after all these years, and the dozens more I was privileged to coach and teach, I don't remember so much about winning or losing. I think about how fortunate I am to have known them.

Regrets? I don't have any.

McHargue a diamond in my backyard
November 6, 2002

A 19th-century philanthropist, the Rev. Russell Conwell, spent much of his life making money, then lived out his remaining years giving it all away. He believed that anyone could make a fortune if he or she just worked hard enough, because wealth was there for the taking. "Acres of diamonds" could be found, he said, if we searched, even in our own backyards.

The good pastor was at least partially correct. I may not have found the big bucks within a few miles of my backdoor this fall, but I did find a diamond in Hubert McHargue.

Hubert is pushing 90 now, but looks more like 70. He reminisces quite a bit about the past too, but much of what he knows has a more modern application. He was an educator for 43 years, coaching basketball for just a handful of them, yet in many ways he's still teaching and coaching.

"As you coach, I think you learn from them [the players] too. You know, you have to prepare them for the future, for a life after basketball. I think coaches are failing in that aspect now. I didn't get out on the floor and cuss. That's for sure. I didn't grab them. I didn't talk nose-to-nose. That doesn't add to the game," McHargue said a few weeks ago in the neat Rosedale home he shares with his wife of 70 years, Kathryn.

McHargue's life has come full circle. He was born in 1913 in tiny Carbon, attended the No. 11 grade school just 300 yards from his house, and graduated from Bridgeton High School in 1931. A baseball star, he lost only one game over his last two years as a pitcher in school, and by 1932 was enrolled at Indiana State Teacher's College (now ISU). His first quarter's tuition: $12.50.

During his summers, McHargue played a little semi-pro baseball, including a stint for a team in Bunsen, now called Universal, in Vermillion County. He first taught at Bellmore in 1935 for $100 a month and after his first year was given the princely raise of an additional $2.50 per month. He soon returned to ISTC to play baseball and earn his bachelor's degree. He pitched for the Sycamores through his senior year, traveling to other state colleges by bus. The team practiced at Memorial Stadium, catching rides to the facility on east Wabash Avenue via Sappington Movers' trucks.

From Bellmore to Coxville to Rosedale, McHargue moved from grade school teacher to grade-school principal to high school English instructor. By 1941, he was a grade school coach at Rosedale, and by 1942, he was head coach for the Hotshots. In 1943, McHargue's squad won the Parke County Tournament by beating Tangier 31-29 at Marshall, no small feat in those days because there were at least 10 schools competing for the title.

"We put full-court pressure on their two big guards. I had a twin set, Marion and Myron Rukes, and we harassed them all over the floor and really slowed them down," Hubert recalled. "They really had a better ballclub than we had, and they were coached by Bill Graves."

McHargue didn't coach long as he had a growing family to feed, and he decided to get into school administration by the end of 1947. But his interest in basketball barely waned over the years.

"Looking back, I regret that I didn't stay in coaching," he said. "Basketball was a fun game then. Now, I think it has become a win game or else."

It had to be fun, but it wasn't always easy. "We played a county team up at Bloomingdale one time, and it was about 20 degrees below zero that night. They had a big coal stove in each end of the gym, and they had to have a guy climb a ladder to keep the score. It was so cold in that place that we couldn't score much—we won 8-6—and we didn't take a shower after the game either," McHargue added.

The coach's two best teams went 18-5, and his '46-'47 squad was one of the best in the area. "We won the county again in '47, and that qualified us for the Wabash Valley tournament in Terre Haute [the Hotshots lost to Palestine]. We also lost to Clinton in the sectional that year, and you know Clinton eventually lost to Shelbyville, the state champ."

"I had so many memorable players from just those few years. One of them was Don Wimsett, a sophomore on my '43 team. He was 6-4, and Branch McCracken came up at least three or four times to watch him play. He [Wimsett] went into the [military] service, by the way, and was coming back with his parents on old Highway 40 to watch my '47 team play and was killed in a car accident. He could have been something else," McHargue said.

"Harry Jukes was another one who could have been a great college player, but he joined the Navy and set some kind of scoring record for them in Japan. He could shoot from all over the floor, but he shot that baby hook too."

McHargue knows that basketball equipment is improved now and that the game is faster paced too, but it's not necessarily better. "I really think the family was more involved in our day because so many schools participated, and it was a county thing then," he said. "With consolidation, you only have a few schools in a county, and you lose the public. That's the main difference."

But the old coach doesn't seem to dwell on the past for long. He still has an eye for the game. "I think one of the main things you have to emphasize in basketball is conditioning," he noted. "You have to be able to run the whole game. On top of that, if the opposition has a weakness, you have to be able to observe it and take advantage of it. That takes scouting. I also believe you should practice all out for an hour and then quit. I think you can over-practice, and kids are burning themselves out."

After McHargue left coaching, he became principal at Clinton Center for a year, then went to Bellmore a second time, then came back to Rosedale to be the principal. He eventually left to teach college-prep sociology and psychology classes at Indianapolis Northwest for a while.

When the winds turn cold, snowbirds Hubert and Kathryn head south to Florida for a while, but one thing is certain: they come back to Parke County to visit old friends and revisit old basketball memories.

Diamonds really do last forever, you know.

It's not science fiction; they're coming…
December 12, 2002

My wife and I have been discussing a room addition to our home for years. We don't want anything spectacular: just an extra bathroom and a few more closets. I'm glad we've waited, though, because a solution to our space problem arrived by Federal Express last week.

You see, my son needed an extra pair of basketball shoes, and we have to special order his. At age 15, he wears a size 16. I may have to mortgage the house to purchase the shoes, but the box they came in, with a little insulation and some plumbing, should come in quite handy as living space.

I've done no polling here and didn't consult anyone in the scientific community, but I have a theory that kids' feet are bigger than they used to be. For example, my son may have a pair of unusually large pods for a boy his age, but he's only one of two players on his basketball team in his class who sport that size. That's two pairs of skis, a good start on a naval armada, dual factors in the slaughter of countless heads of cattle—in one freshman class.

I don't exactly have a pair of clodhoppers designed for ballet myself; I wear a size 12 and have done so since I was in the eighth grade. As a matter of fact, I had a bit of a complex about my big feet by age 14 or so. I was convinced that when combined with a pair of straight-legged pants, my feet surpassed sore thumbs in the being-noticed department. I felt like I belonged in a Warner Brothers cartoon, but now big feet are apparently a status symbol, something like having built-in designer snowshoes.

Sadly, I can't even wear the shoes my son discards as hand-me-downs or garage sale fodder unless I get used to wearing three extra pairs of socks or getting used to what I call the "Munchkin Look." That's where the toes of one's shoes curl up due to a lack of occupants.

Apparently, my "Expanding Feet Theorem" is not without some merit. I didn't consult a podiatrist, but I did speak to the people who sell athletic shoes for a living. One of them is Marsha Nasser, who's been fitting shoes at Pacesetter Sports for 10 years. She too thinks kids are flashing a few inches more foot these days.

"Oh, I believe their feet are bigger now," Nasser said, "but I think it's because people are buying more shoes for their kids and, consequently, their feet can grow to their potential. I'm 50, and when I was a kid you didn't get new shoes until the shoes you had were pinching your feet. Now that's not always the case."

Some may feel that better health care and nutrition are the cause of expanding feet, but Nasser doesn't buy that idea.

"I don't think we're feeding them [kids] better," she said. "As a matter of fact, we're feeding them terribly. We're buying them shoes, and more of them. In

Japan, they used to bind women's feet to make them smaller, and in a way, the same thing happened to our children years ago. But now, parents here buy shoes often just because their kids want them. We want to make our kids happy."

I can relate to Nasser's ideas. I used to wear my "sneaks" until they disintegrated. By the time I gave them up, the typical soles on my shoes looked like Indy-car tires. Since my parents weren't exactly rolling in money, I held back a little on asking for that new pair of Chuck Taylors or Beta Bullets.

Bill Liebler, who sells shoes for Kessler's Sports, doesn't really have an idea as to why bigger feet are common; he simply agrees that they are bigger and may be getting bigger still.

The sizes are definitely changing," Liebler said. "We're putting kids in bigger shoes now, and that's not because they're buying the shoes too big. We used to go out to schools with a 'gut size' of about 10 or so. That was the average size that kids wore, even many of our college players. Now, the most popular size is about a 12, and that's often middle school."

He added, "Girls' feet don't seem to be getting much bigger, although they don't seem to balk nearly as much as they used to about wearing their proper size. I think girls are more in tone with buying shoes that fit than in just what looks good."

Liebler went on to suggest that perhaps better strength and conditioning programs may be feeding our kids' feet. "Whatever it is, I do know that shoe companies used to stop making half-sizes after 13, but they've changed that."

I walked through the house this afternoon and caught bits and pieces of a conversation my son was having with my wife at the kitchen table. In between bites of what turned out to be the last remaining scraps of food in our refrigerator, he told his mom that he thinks he needs a new pair of shoes; the low-cuts he's wearing to school are rubbing his heels.

A few minutes later, I found myself thumbing through the last few dollars in my wallet and contemplating yet another shoe box arriving on my front step in a week or so. Then, I had an idea.

Maybe buying those shoes isn't such a financial strain after all. It's an investment. I'll need to buy a burial vault someday; I can plan to build that pontoon boat I've always wanted; I'll have that carport I've been thinking about. Why, I'm saving money in the long run.

Please, keep telling me that.

A professor at the top of his game
January 29, 2003

An exasperated student walked out of one of Don Layton's history classes a few years ago threatening to blow up the Indiana State University professor's car. Wearing his best deadpan expression, Layton advised the boy to be careful not to burn his lips on the car's exhaust pipe in the attempt.

I've always known that Layton was one of the best teachers I ever had and one of the funniest men I ever met. What I didn't know until I came across an old black-and-white photo in a book on Oscar Robertson a few years ago was that Layton was also a top-drawer basketball player in his high school days almost 50 years ago, and behind all of his lessons and jokes was an even better story.

Layton has been at ISU since 1963. He's spent his years in Terre Haute teaching one of the most popular classes on campus about World War II and his beloved specialty, the history of Russia. His irreverent jokes about Eva Braun, about Feodor, the bell- ringing czar, and just about anything and anyone else, sometimes mask what I already knew: Layton knows his stuff.

At 5 feet, 11 inches and 130 pounds, the pencil-thin Layton played at Indianapolis Howe from 1951 to 1955. Since freshmen couldn't play varsity basketball in those days, he labored to help his squad achieve an undefeated season, a first for his school. But it was his senior year that held the most memories for Layton, as did the recollections of facing one of the best players in the history of the sport.

"I'm reluctant to judge myself as a player," Layton says. "I was a pretty good shooter, although in those days that meant the ability to hit 15-foot shots. I was also pretty quick and was able to squirm loose a lot for shots near the basket. Our team played a 1-2-2 zone, and I was the point man. When opponents shot, I released. I scored a lot of points on breakaways that way, and I also stole the ball a lot."

Indianapolis sportswriter Bob Williams, who once called Layton "wiry," also said the future professor was the most underrated player in the city. The captain of his team and a four-year starter on the baseball team, Layton was a candidate for the Indianapolis high school athlete of the year in 1955. He lost out to Shortridge's Jim Lohr.

"I always played hard, dove for the ball, went into the stands for it, and gave my all on the court. But at the same time, I had fun, and except for the City Tournament against [Crispus) Attucks, never took the game too seriously," Layton says.

About facing the immortal "The Big O," Layton didn't bother to hide his admiration. "Robertson was by far the best player I ever went up against and probably the best I ever saw, although it is a toss up between him and [Larry] Bird. He was like a man among boys, and I always had the feeling that he could score whenever he wished. He had an amazing court awareness, and he also had an impressive team with him," Layton said. He added that Willie Merriweather went on to Purdue and Sharrick Mitchell played at Butler. Two other Attucks players also had fine careers at Indiana Central.

"I would emphasize that all of these players were gentlemen, as was their coach, Ray Crowe. The games against them were hard but always clean, and sportsmanship was always emphasized by their team," Layton said.

He recalled facing Robertson in the Indianapolis City Tournament in his senior season: "Going into the city tournament, we had lost only one game—to Connersville in their gym, a bandbox if I ever saw one. I was one of the top scorers in the city and county, and we thought we had a good chance to win. I spent a lot of time double-teaming Oscar on the press, and we held him to under 20, but we lost by 13. That was the worst game of organized basketball I ever played on offense. I had one point. It wasn't that I was missing shots; I just wasn't getting any of them," he said.

"Most of my family from around the state came to that game at the Butler Fieldhouse, and I felt humiliated. I went home and went to bed afterward, not talking to any of them. The next time we played Attucks, I got 17 points, but we were blown out, and Oscar broke the career scoring record for Indianapolis. Remember, he was only a junior. Incidentally, my senior year, we also played and beat Terre Haute Garfield and Clinton."

Looking back at the evolution of basketball, as a history teacher might, Layton makes it clear that he doesn't like many of the changes that he's seen. "I have always believed that athletics are means to ends, not ends in themselves. There are, of course, many things that one learns from sports that are applicable to life: teamwork, decision making, sacrifice, hard work and responsibility. Today, it seems that so many people are no longer willing to take responsibility for their own actions—blaming someone else for their mistakes. Just witness the lawsuits by people blaming McDonald's for their being overweight or casinos for gambling addictions. In sports, you have to take responsibility for your actions. If you make a mistake, it is visible for everyone. You can't hide from it."

Layton also doesn't like the fact that basketball is so much more physical. "When I played, it was a non-contact sport. This is, obviously, no longer the case, and I don't like that. I also don't like the obvious lack of fundamentals in the game. If I were a coach, I would make all of my players watch the movie "Hoosiers" to see the importance of teamwork and fundamentals. To see the exact opposite, I would have them watch tapes of the United States in the World Basketball Championships in Indy last summer."

Layton went on to say that he's happy women are so much more involved in basketball, that he doesn't like class basketball since he played before crowds up to 15,000 in the only sectional in Indianapolis, and that schools like ISU still best reflect the positive features of athletics.

"I am truly amazed when I go to the Verizon Athletic/Academic award banquet and see what truly outstanding students many of our athletes are," Layton said. In fact, it was Layton's unabiding love for books and learning that eventually beat out his desire to continue with basketball after high school. He turned down an offer to play at Butler to attend school at DePauw.

"I didn't play basketball when I went to DePauw," Layton said. "I went there on a Rector Scholarship, which was for academics. Nevertheless, I also had to work to supplement that scholarship since my father had died when I was 16, and my family had very little money, and certainly none to help me get through college. I was the first in our family to go to college, and I was so afraid that I would flunk out that I devoted nearly all of my time to my studies."

Layton's work paid off. He made Phi Beta Kappa, but he never really strayed far from basketball either. "I did work a bit with the DePauw coach when I went there, Cal Luther, who later left and had an illustrious career at Murray State. He was by far the smartest coach I ever had contact with."

Layton still follows basketball, although not the pros, "whose game only approximates basketball as I knew it." He's held season tickets at Indiana State from the time he began teaching there. It's the hope of many students that he'll be teaching for a good while longer too.

A few years ago, I stood staring at a shelf of shaving cream at a local grocery store. Next to me, a stooped store clerk stocked razor blades. Don Layton waltzed by me and said, just loudly enough for the boy to hear, "Still have that shoplifting problem, Lunsford?"

He just kept walking up the aisle as I put what I had in my hand back on the shelf. Don Layton had struck again.

Watching Superman play basketball
February 14, 2003

My son and I both broke our mutually-imposed morning silence at nearly the same instance a few days ago when we noticed that the sun was up just a little earlier than usual as we made our way to school. We are early risers, and our daily grind the past few months has been spent, for most part, in the darkness and cold.

But now we are gradually seeing changes in the coming of the new days; changes that are as welcome as a pair of well-worn hightops on our feet. I've been told that I am growing nostalgic in my middle years. That may very well be true, but I don't think we take much time out of our business these days to notice little things that, in the long run, reflect big changes in who and what we are.

It wasn't the rising sun, but its setting that caught my attention one evening not long ago as I drove toward another school in another county to watch my son, now a gangly, freckled freshman, play in a basketball game.

Heading across a hilly country road in the crystal blue February twilight, I sat behind the wheel seeing the pavement ahead but remembering the times 35 years ago when I traveled the same way in the backseat of my aunt and uncle's Chevy, the falling snow flickering across the headlamps.

In those days, I hitched rides with them with a dollar in my pocket as they headed out in the early evening to my cousin Roger's games. I wasn't a well-traveled kid in those days—didn't know anyone who was—so when we walked into the smoky box kiln of the Staunton gym as Rog was warming up to face the Yellow Jackets, or negotiated the oak in the middle of the road before joining up with the old Rio Grande on its way to Van Buren to take on the Blue Devils, it seemed as though I had stepped past the ticket booths into other worlds.

My cousin was a 6-foot-4, curly-headed licorice whip, and he was the closest thing to Superman to ever come my way. I used to wander across the road to his house, mosey through his room, glide my hands across his trophies, and wait for him to come home from practice or work, just to see him, just to soak up who and what he was. My first basketball was an old Voit, rubbed slick on the concrete pad in front of his garage, its orange hide turned a chalky peach by a million bounces back to our hands.

He played at Rosedale for a tall and talented team, but unfortunately, at a time when small-school powerhouses, like Cloverdale and Bainbridge, were nearly unbeatable. It seemed as if, in spite of all of their triumphs and all the cheers they experienced, that team was destined to be disappointed, an also-ran that came tantalizingly close at the season's end.

Whether he won or lost mattered. It mattered to that little town, and it mattered to my aunt and uncle, who were often tense and silent before a game, either depressed or ecstatic afterward. It was as if their world's ability to spin on an axis depended on that single Friday night game in Clinton or Rockville. Everything, from the pre-game chili in the school cafeteria to the seat we chose before tip-off (my uncle preferred to be near the floor so he could let the referees know he was there), seemed to point our compass toward that single instant when we saw my cousin and his teammates pour from the locker room in the black and gold, their scratchy wool warm-ups still zipped to the neck as they heard "On Wisconsin" for the first time that night.

I remember how folks lingered in the gym after the games, the post-game desserts we ate as we waited for the players to finish their showers and head down the narrow, lockered hallway with their hair still wet and dripping on their letter jackets. I admired those players who now have middle-aged paunches, graying beards, and balding heads. I still admire them.

Now, I fear, we exalt the future first-round picks whose high school games are covered by the national networks, whose ineligibilities and promises of big money seem to dwarf the reasons why we ever started to play the game in the first place. Instead, we've made basketball a year-round job for many of our kids, and we have seventh graders promised shoe contracts.

A friend told me just a week ago about a Web site where he could read about the best eighth-grade talent in America, and how they rank with other 14-year-olds around the country. Eighth graders...

Times aren't like they were in that wonderful age when I saw my cousin as a hero, but I've cautioned my own son to guard not only his man, but also what he does, what he says, and how he handles himself. Someone else's son will be watching him.

I believe every man can be a superman. I believe that because one used to live across the road from me.

The best little big man who never played
February 26, 2003

At the exact time that I write this column, a full week before it is to appear in print, Michael Kor is finding his seat at Mackey Arena in West Lafayette. Tonight, his beloved Purdue Boilermakers take on the Michigan Wolverines, and there is no place in the world that this incredible little man would rather be.

As Michael—"Mickey" to his friends—says, "Tonight, when I go to the game, I'll forget everything. I'll forget all that happened to me, for a while."

What happened to Mickey isn't a new story at all; his is nearly the exact same tale experienced by millions of people. The only difference in his story is that he lived to tell it. Eleven million others didn't.

Michael Kor is a Holocaust survivor. He was born in Latvia, experienced life in the ghettos there, lost his family there, spent six months in the nauseating hull of a rusting freighter in the Baltic Sea and the claustrophobic darkness of a cattle train box car in East Prussia. He lived the horror over three more years in the death camp at Magdeburg, Germany, spending his long days as a slave laborer, shoving and pulling boxes of ammunition under the watchful eyes of armed guards and their vicious dogs. That was over 60 years ago, a lot of water under the bridge. But the water still runs sluggishly and smells of death.

"Life isn't smooth, but I never gave up," Kor told my students as they stood with their eyes trained on the tiny man in his gold Purdue fisherman's cap and gray Boilermakers' basketball sweatshirt. The class had come to listen to him speak at the C.A.N.D.L.E.S. Holocaust Museum in Terre Haute a week ago.

"More important than sports, than VCRs, and televisions, is freedom and having a chance to live," he says.

At age 13, Kor was removed from the Riga ghetto. It was the winter of 1941. He can never forget the last day he saw his mother, who, Michael says, "must have seen something I didn't when the Nazis came. She pushed me away from her side, told me to tell them that I was older, that I could work. She saved my life."

He can't forget how the Nazis sprayed salty water through the hatches to the thirsty prisoners below the decks of the ship, laughing at what they saw. "They thought it was funny that we stood there with our mouths open like little birds, just trying to get some of that water," he said.

Until his liberation, Kor clung to life while so many others gave up. Despite years of reflection, he has no explanation as to why he survived the daily camp selections. "They [Nazi guards] would line us up, and then they'd give us a number. Then, they'd take all the twos one day, or all of the numbers divisible by two the next. I was always the number they didn't want. I don't know why."

When freedom did come in 1945, it was in the form of the American Army, the 250th Engineer Combat

Battalion, and Lt. Col. Andrew Nehf, who just happened to be from Terre Haute. Kor was cleaned up, fattened up, given a uniform to wear, and was soon the outfit's interpreter.

"I could speak German and Russian. I was no genius, but I began to pick up English. They put a GI uniform on me, and I looked like a little mascot," he says. "I used to imagine what freedom would look like when I was a prisoner," Kor adds. "The day I was liberated, a soldier walked over to a mess truck and handed me a bottle of Coca-Cola. I thought freedom looked like a bottle of Coca-Cola."

Kor didn't want to immigrate to Israel after the war as so many other displaced survivors did, although he did meet his wife, Eva, who suffered at Auschwitz, there in 1960. "I wanted to go to America. I wanted to come here because everyone is equal here. Hope is a beautiful thing for a human being to have," he says.

Nehf saw to it that Kor came to Terre Haute, and Mickey promptly attended State High, then completed two years at Indiana State. From there, he went on to Purdue, from which he graduated with a degree in pharmacy. By 1952, Kor was in an American GI's uniform again, but this time as a soldier in the closing months of the Korean War.

"I was proud to be in the Army as a real soldier," he says, "not as a toy soldier this time."

I guess that's where I could have started this whole story, with Mickey Kor graduating from Purdue and becoming a dyed-in-the-wool Boilermakers fan who never misses a game, who gently ribs Indiana University supporters, and who can recite the glory of Purdue sports and the coaching philosophy of Gene Keady chapter-and-verse.

The story could have been about how the diminutive 74-year-old man, who often sprinkles sports metaphors in his conversations, who says of himself that he's "in the game's final five minutes" as far as life goes, just wants to go to Purdue's games now, because "I've worked my whole life, really."

That could have been the whole story, but it isn't. Let's hope Michael Kor gets an extra overtime period or two tacked on to his extraordinary life.

He has a lot left to tell us.

Writer walking his way toward the season
October 15, 2003

As I often do in the early evening, I took a walk a few nights ago along our country road to stretch my legs and clear my head. It took no longer than a few minutes, and a little sweat, for me to slip back into time. The western sun occasionally forced my head down toward the summer-baked pavement, but I could clearly see the road ahead, and the years behind me.

It doesn't seem possible that it has been so long ago, but I clearly remembered walking, or running, or riding my brother's old Schwinn, along a similar road. It was in early fall, just before organized basketball practice was to start, that I often took off after mowing grass or throwing school books aside, to cover the three miles down the county line to Rosedale to shoot buckets at the park or get in a pick-up game at the old gym. The latter place was a dimly-lit affair, its floor warped by a water leak, its odor a mixture of old bleachers, old sweat, and undoubtedly older dust.

In even younger days, I used to sometimes sit in an old lawn chair and watch my cousin and his friends play by the light of a single bulb on my aunt and uncle's concrete drive. I'd walk across the road and watch as those gods, not much older than my son is now, rattled home jumpers off a plywood backboard.

Now, I walk to keep my joints lubricated and my desk chair-conditioned backside from moving into wider pants, but if I walk just far enough, it feels as though I could be playing again. I'm not an old man, but not a young one anymore either, and the thought of blowing out a knee or wounding my pride in an "adult" league somewhere seems unlikely. I am, however, of an age when the falling leaves, bronze soybean fields, and the rustling of the October corn stalks makes me a bit nostalgic. But more than that, I'm anticipating a new season, not a dying one.

There's more than a hint of change in the air this week, marked by the folks I've seen in sweaters and wearing long sleeves, and in a way, change is one reason I look forward to fall basketball. At a time when most associate the weather with an ending, the opening of the practice season suggests something just beginning. That something could eventually be a team that struggles to put things together all winter, only to play its best ball by the sectional tournament. But, it's just as likely to be a squad that peaks too early and leaves fans waiting for next year. Either way, every school, every coach, and every player gets to start over in a few weeks when they roll out the basketballs to break in their new shoes and high hopes.

I too get a fresh start each year with this column. I'd like to think I'm a little like that second-string guard who's spent the summer working on a weak left hand or polishing a jump shot. That is, I get another chance to do things right this season. I'm determined too, but positive that I'll have both good days and bad.

I've learned a few things about my writing over the years, and one of them is to wait on the best stories to sit next to me in the bleachers, show up in my mailbox, or stop me in the grocery store. I've met the most remarkable people through this column, and I have no reason to believe it won't just keep happening.

I'm a blue jeans and T-shirt kind of guy, and those are the kind of stories—a bit disheveled, but comfortable—that readers should expect again this year: a baseball tale of woe and devotion; a piece on the importance of dreams; the best of locker room inspiration; the coaches who most influenced other coaches; and, of course, a few stories about the Pizza Hut Wabash Valley Classic, the tournament to which I am now most certainly addicted.

For now, it's watching the leaves of my scarlet oak drop in the yard, keeping my gutters clean, and watching my Red Sox go as far as fate will take them. If there's another thing my walking time has also taught me, it's that the best things are worth waiting for, and I see no reason to rush the combines, the heavy frosts, and the first "killers" to be run in practice; they'll take care of themselves.

As I walk, I often dodge the dogs, the ditches, and the cars that speed down the road. I've learned to pay attention, least my exercise be the kind that hurts. I'm noticing now that the sassafras reds and the tulip poplar golds are going to be as pretty as in any of the best falls I can recall.

That's one thing I love about this time of the year: While I'm busy remembering how good times used to be, I know that the best things are yet to come.

Big dreams are still worth having
November 12, 2003

My 10-year-old nephew, Nick, is a little guy with a big dream. It wasn't but a few weeks ago that he confided in my wife and me about his goal: Buying a motor scooter that costs $1,600. That's the approximate value of 10 cars like the first jalopy I owned.

"That's a lot of money, Nick," my wife cautioned, knowing that his fashionably middle-class parents aren't about to fork over that kind of serious cash, even at Christmas, and that Nick's being able to raise the money himself anytime soon is somewhere between impossible and "Let's hope he just forgets about it."

But Nick told her that he was already investing in a savings plan that would make the purchase of the scooter possible without the need of his parents putting money in the project at all. So, somewhere, buried in my brother-in-law's yard in an undisclosed county just north of Terre Haute, is Nick's secret scooter fund: 75 cents of hard-earned currency awaiting the other $1,599.25 that he plans to scrape up by doing odd jobs and hunting under sofa cushions after company leaves.

At his current rate of saving, Nick may not get the scooter until he gets a senior citizen discount on the thing, but I am confident that he'll work pretty hard for a long time before he ever considers giving up on the dream, if he ever does.

As in Nick's case, a lot of the former athletes that I talk with—most admittedly well past their prime—seem to have had similar experiences in working toward their successes a long time before they ever enjoyed the glories of cutting down nets, caressing trophies, or doing media interviews. But that kind of life is sounding old-school these days.

I hear that ESPN plans to continue to broadcast high-profile high school basketball games this year, particularly in the wake of LeBron James' television successes last season. One of those games will pit a nationally ranked Los Angeles high school team against one from Louisiana. That's a pretty long road trip on a school night, isn't it?

Larry Bird, who hasn't been off the court that long, but who now seems to come from a long-lost era of sports heroes pictured in rickety, out-of-focus highlight reels, once said, "My mother worked a lot of hours; always double shifts. We used her paycheck to pay for food, and my dad's check to pay all of our bills, and we just barely got by. I think that's the way everyone should grow up."

Read one of the armfuls of biographies about Bird, and you'll soon learn that he came from a childhood of poverty, that he didn't have the newest shoes, the best practice gear, the money to attend high- profile camps. Instead he just played in parks, in pick-up games, and anytime the gym doors opened. He played against bigger and better players until he was bigger and definitely better himself.

Not surprisingly, that's pretty much the same way it happened for Oscar Robertson and Bobby Plump years earlier, and later for Damon Bailey too. An endless list of others, both great and good, even mediocre players, probably wouldn't trade their similarly tough experiences in poorly lit gyms with worn-out shoes and netless rims for later glories. As a matter of fact, I'd be willing to bet that they now wear those tougher times like medals.

I know we can't go back. Praying for an age when kids shot at hoops nailed up in the lofts of countryside barns, when they played by themselves in the cold of frozen backyard courts, or when they played pick-up baseball games in sandlots under the watchful eyes of parents who had the sense to stay at the kitchen sink window ... well, perhaps we can't get there anymore. I'm certainly glad we can't go back to the Cold War, McCarthyism and polio either.

But when it comes to sports, we may be trying to do too much for our kids. A long-dead poet once said that we all need to "learn to labor and to wait," but waiting isn't fashionable anymore. Instead, it seems as though we're in a rush, not to fulfill a dream, but to grab the loot and run.

Nick, keep dreaming and keep saving, buddy. Getting that scooter is going to take what many of us lack anymore. It may be called gumption, get-up-and-go, or grit, but whatever it is, it's worth having as much or more than anything you can buy.

Winds of change just keep blowing
November 12, 2003

Shivering in the cold of a Friday night football game last weekend, I knew by the score on the board at the south end of the field that the next set of bleachers I'd be nestled onto would be those in a warm gymnasium. As sure as the cold blast of Arctic air that smacked me across the face that night, the wind signaled to me that one season was coming to a close, but another is but a matter of days away.

Being an English teacher, I'm supposed to be able to see things symbolically, and to me, the fall wind always seems to blow away the summer doldrums and usher in a fresh basketball season. Several schools in the Valley have already played their jamborees and girls box scores will show up on the sports pages this week.

Virtually every coach in the area is undoubtedly already losing a little sleep, and I imagine there are a number of players whose biggest concerns aren't chemistry or algebra anymore; it's keeping their lunches down through another late afternoon of wind sprints and shuffle drills.

In his travelogue "Home Country," the great Ernie Pyle wrote about that Midwest wind and what it meant to him. In his first chapter, Home in Indiana, the Dana native wrote, "It [the wind] comes from so far and blows so gently and yet so restlessly; it rustles the leaves and the branches of the maple trees in a sort of symphony of sadness, and it doesn't pass on and leave them still. It just keeps coming, like the infinite flow of Old Man River."

That steady and persistent wind has been blowing Hoosiers toward and through basketball seasons for generations now. The IHSAA invented itself in 1903, but the game had been played in Indiana for a while before that. Its inventor, James Naismith, laid down the first set of rules in 1892, and we know that the first scheduled basketball game in Indiana was played at the Crawfordsville YMCA in March 1894. Incidentally, the host Y team beat a squad from Lafayette 45-21 in that contest. The winds of change have blown through the sport ever since.

There were only 15 member schools in the IHSAA's first year, and it took until 1911 to get the first state tournament organized. Crawfordsville had the distinction of winning that first title too, but tiny Wingate, led by the game's first superstar, Homer Stonebraker, was perhaps the state's first dominant team, winning the championship in 1913 and 1914. Franklin's "Wonder Five" won three straight championships starting in 1920, and by 1924, one of the state's greatest players ever, Johnny Wooden, led Martinsville to its first state crown.

I don't think too many folks then, even while they were building the biggest gymnasiums in the country to hold the incredible crowds who were packing them, could envision the game as it's played today. In the very old days, the odd kid out used a broom handle to poke the ball back out of the burlap sack the players hung from an iron barrel hoop, and jump balls were used after every score. Break-away rims and gel-filled shoes weren't quite in the picture yet

It's obvious that the game we always seem to see in the nostalgic light of Milan's Indians, cheer sweaters, and Chuck Taylors has changed. If most rule changes were mere cool drafts, then the introduction of class basketball was a tornado, and those of us whose lives have spanned the gap between the two eras are left to wonder what's in store for the game next.

Local attorney, Craig McKee, an ardent non-class advocate, eloquently speaks of the fragile heritage we seemed to have committed to the dustbins of the past when class became a reality.

"I feel distant from basketball today because high school basketball has lost its specialness, and its athletes now move ceaselessly from season to season to season without an appreciation of basketball history or the meaning of the state tournament," McKee says.

He added, "As I have contended from the beginning, school sports, combined with AAU, and all the other opportunities for team play, have created a glut of trophies and events, in ignorance of this law: 'Nothing becomes more valuable by its reproduction.' It was the rarity of the trophy, the near impossibility of earning it, that made it seem so valuable."

The game many of us used to know may have changed like the direction of that unpredictable Indiana wind. We may not like many of those changes— I know I don't—but I have about as much power to stop them as I do holding back the breezes that blow from the west across the cornfields near my house. I've had to make peace with those gusts of change.

I'm still pretty content watching just about anybody play basketball, although I know I'd rather watch two very average junior high school teams than a pair of elite NBA squads. Most of all, I'm just anxious to get started watching this imperfect but essential part of our lives as it unfolds on the hardwood each weekend night this winter.

I guess that when it comes to this remarkable game of ours, an old proverb best applies to me: "It doesn't matter which way the wind blows as long as I get a breeze."

Making the grade isn't always easy
December 10, 2003

I have a friend—let's call him Sam—who like me, has taught a number of years. Like many veteran teachers, he has the annoying habit of grading everything, just as if he were permanently affixed to that desk chair of his. A red marking pen has become his metaphor for life; he even grades my columns.

Sam doesn't teach English and isn't that fond of reading, so when I wrote a column last year about my favorite basketball books, he hated it. "It's a C at best, maybe a D+" he said. "It had no point to it, no zip."

I can just hear him at home talking to his wife: "I found a little dust under the couch last night, dear. That's a C- in vacuuming…" Or, "That new hair coloring of yours just doesn't quite cut it, does it? I'll give it a C+."

I also wonder how he rates sleeping with his collie and house cat on the couch in the basement.

I'm not, however, exactly stung by his criticism. He's no connoisseur of great literature—I suspect he knows TV Guide better than "Seinfeld's" Frank Castanza —but before I dismiss him as either slightly eccentric (or slightly cracked), I remember that he also often makes one other point, and this one has some merit.

"You don't always say what you want to say," he tells me. "Why don't you really tell people what you mean?"

"For instance?" I ask.

"Well, you know it, and I know it. Adults have taken a lot of fun out of sports. Can you remember that when we were kids we settled a lot of our own disputes, made our own calls, spent time in the gym or at the park on our own in pick-up games? No one made us do it. There were no summer leagues or extra coaches. The IHSAA wouldn't let you do much that was organized," he said.

"Kids play too many organized games now, they play too much in the summer. They're burning out; they quit playing in school, and now, a lot of coaches are pushing them to pick just one sport. We're taking this whole sports business too seriously; not every kid is going to be a college or pro athlete. It's supposed to be fun. I know you feel that way too," he says.

If my old friend had read a piece in Time Magazine in late October, he'd know what Garland Allen, a fitness director in Ridgewood, New Jersey schools said. "We're creating a generation that is over-scheduled by parents, over-tested by teachers, and over-trained by coaches."

After a reasonably lengthy tirade in which Sam went on to add that I need to recommend that fans bone up on rules, that many officials need to realize folks aren't paying for a ticket to watch them make calls, and that I should quit telling him that his belt and shoes should match, he bluntly asks, "What do you think? Am I right or not?"

Just maybe he is, but I'm giving him a B-. I can be

a tough grader too.

Cold weather warmed by memories of coaches
February 4, 2004

It's pretty safe to say that quite a number of teachers working in classrooms today are there because they had a teacher or two who inspired them to be educators. That's certainly true in my case. Lloyd Bodie, a junior high science teacher, made me want to spend my life at the chalkboard; I'll never forget him.

That same idea seems to apply to basketball coaches too, and that theory was reinforced after I spoke to a pair of local coaching legends about who inspired them to dedicate their lives to a game and the boys who play it.

Jim Jones and Pat Rady have coached basketball for a lot of years. Whether it be at Springs Valley or Terre Haute North, Bainbridge or Terre Haute South, the pair has more than 1,200 wins and about 80 years of hardwood experience between them. Both have pretty good ballclubs again this year too.

"One of my first influences was my father," Jones said, "but I suppose Branch McCracken and Adolph Rupp were the first coaches who had an influence on my coaching. I believe Coach Knight [Bob] and Coach Wooden [John] have been the most influential though."

Jones had watched what the UCLA mentor had done for years, but meeting him impressed him more. "I had the opportunity to run into Coach Wooden about 30 years ago in Louisville in the lobby of a hotel. He was such a cordial individual, and I mentioned to him that I hadn't read his book ["Practical Modern Basketball"].

Well, after he went back to the West Coast, he got a copy of the book and mailed it to me with a personal note."

The Patriots' coach saw Wooden again last December in Indianapolis and reminded the legendary UCLA teacher of his kindness so many years ago. "I just now really got to thank him," Jones said.

Jones went on to mention the influence others have had on him.

"When I was at Springs Valley, I learned so much from Jack Butcher at Loogootee and Sam Alford at South Knox, but especially from Guy Glover at Bloomfield. I worked basketball camps with him; what a great Christian man he was."

He added, "Coaching is a continuous process. It's all about getting better and working at it. These men helped teach me that."

Not to be left off his list of mentors is Jones' wife, Joyce. "She hasn't taught me the X's and 0's, but more of how I should conduct myself, and I really appreciate that," he said.

Pat Rady didn't hesitate when asked about his mentors: "Ed Orrill, my high school coach at Roachdale, and 'Dutch' R.F. Struck, the athletic director at Hanover College," he said.

Rady can't tell enough stories about Orrill. Even as we walked toward our cars after our talk, the Braves' coach related to me how Orrill may very well be the biggest influence in his life.

"His knowledge of the game was incredible—he was ahead of his time, actually," Rady said. "Mr. Orrill treated me like I was important. When I was a junior in high school, he let me coach the sixth-grade team, and he taught me how to scout too." Rady went on to say, "I began keeping a notebook way back in high school, and I'd write down anything that I thought would be helpful to me. You know, to me, Ed Orrill will always be 'Coach.' I really don't know where I'd be without him, you know, what I would have become."

After Rady's high school playing days were over, he headed to Hanover to play basketball and was promptly cut from the team. "I told Coach Orrill that I might as well forget about coaching basketball because I wasn't playing it. He told me, 'Who said you had to be a player to coach? You have to be a student of the game.' I took that to heart, and, well, I made the team next year too."

Struck's influence on Rady was a bit more subtle, but important nonetheless. "He showed me the value of being a schooled man, the values of life," Rady said.

It's obvious that the Braves' coach, and his counterpart in North Terre Haute, would like to think they're passing those same qualities on to their players.

Just a few days ago, I ran into Tom Rohr, one of the best basketball officials in the Wabash Valley. For some reason, we too arrived at the subject of basketball mentors. Tom, who is undoubtedly in as good of physical shape as he was as a high school senior, played for Bernard Gideon at Montezuma and said the lessons he learned from Gideon influenced him for the rest of his life.

"Coach taught us to be disciplined," Rohr said. "He always had a curfew through the week during basketball season, and I kept it. He'd sometimes call my house around nine o'clock, and I'd already be in bed. My mom would tell him that I was asleep, but he'd still tell her he had to speak to me. Later, when I coached some junior high ball, I had a curfew too."

That's not all of Rohr's story. On one particular night before his undefeated Aztecs played at Brazil, he saw one of his players—he only had six—out past the curfew. The next day, Rohr sat him down for much of the game. They lost their only game of the year.

"Hey, if there's anything I learned from my coach, it's that I'd do what I said I'd do."

Somewhere, I'm sure, there are a few old coaches around who can appreciate that.

You don't need Ralphie for a real Christmas story
December 24, 2004

You've probably seen "A Christmas Story," the classic holiday movie about Ralphie, the Ovaltine decoder ring-reading little Hoosier whose greatest goal in life is getting a Red Ryder bb-gun under his tree on Christmas morning.

I think the film has become such a favorite of my generation, not because we've all been warned, "You'll shoot yer eye out kid," but because it takes us back to simpler times; times when we had downtown shopping, buckle-on snow boots, and Davy Crockett coon-skin caps (even though the one in the movie belonged to villain Scott Farkus).

We felt safer living in those days, perhaps more optimistic; certainly less cynical. Like Ralphie, I remember heading into town with my parents to pick out a Christmas tree on a corner lot lit by strings of colored bulbs. We too had a cantankerous old furnace that popped and belched smoke; I even had an aunt who had a penchant for unusual gifts too.

Memories are magical, powerful things, and they don't have to be about favorite Christmases to be special. True, I can still remember my Fort Apache cowboy and Indian set, my Fred Flintstone punching bag, my Dick Butkus simulated-autograph, synthetic leather football. I recall the black-and-white tile floor of our front porch, and the scent of pine from the tree that we kept there, even the frost that formed on the inside of the multi-paned windows on the coldest of nights. I can still see our orange and red glass bubble lights, the strings of tinsel, and our collie who liked to sleep next to the tree. But, perhaps above all, I remember a promise that my dad made to me one Christmas. He said that when it warmed up a bit, he'd put up a basketball goal for me. He eventually lived up to his word, and the orange rubber basketball I had under the tree that winter was soon a mud-splattered mess when the goalpost went into the ground that February.

My first basketball court was a patch of dirt near my grandfather's garden, and I can't begin to calculate how many hours I spent on that little spot of soil worn smooth by a million dribbles, how many imaginary last-second shots I hit, how many championships I won there. I do know that I wouldn't trade the time I spent there for anything.

When I ask others about their best basketball memories, I usually get immediate responses. The game has a way of sustaining itself in our heads and our hearts. For example, as I sat at a worktable grading papers nearly a week ago on the last day of school before Christmas break, I asked fellow teacher and former coach, Sheldon Oberholzter, to reminisce a bit.

Oberholtzer won a sectional title at Montezuma in 1982, the first for that school in nearly 30 years, and I expected he'd drop a name or game from those days. Instead, the former Patricksburg Bulldog remembered a game he saw in the late 50s while he was an assistant coach at Van Buren.

It was in the old Brazil High School gymnasium, and the host Red Devils were playing their nemesis, the Staunton Yellow Jackets. As a whistle signaled a stop in the action, the ball rolled toward Brazil's coach, Jim Hannah. In those days the team benches were located at one end of the gym, and since Hannah wasn't particularly pleased that Staunton was given possession, he zipped the ball to the Yellow Jackets' coach, Whitey Roeschlein. The Staunton coach took offense and drilled the ball back to Hannah, and as the packed house screamed, the two coaches continued to play burnout before a referee interceded.

Two days after watching Sheldon tell his story with a smile, I sat at our church eating our annual Christmas breakfast and listened to Milbrey Huxford tell me about her late husband, Wayne, who played for the 1939 Rosedale team.

She clearly remembered how good Wayne's team was, and how she was certain that they had made it pretty far in the old Valley Tournament. Sure enough, when I looked at the records, I confirmed that the Hot Shots had made the final 16 teams, and Wayne had scored six points in a 33-20 win over Wheatland in a Friday morning game. I know that those memories are special to Milbrey.

As is the case for the grown-up Ralphie, who narrates The Christmas Story, we can't go back to the days of our youth, and, hopefully, we're a little too smart to stick our tongues on frozen flagpoles.

But, when we open our gifts tomorrow morning, we'll know that many of our favorite presents aren't even under the tree; they've already happened.

What I remember about Larry Bird
February 25, 2004

When I think of Larry Bird, I still see his scabbed, knobby knees, his mane of blonde hair, and his crooked little finger that forced him to shoot a basketball like a dainty old lady drinking properly from her teacup. I see him hitch his already short shorts up by sliding his thumbs inside his waistband, and I can still see him step back from the free-throw line after a make, wipe the sweat from his face with the back of a forearm, and then go back to make another.

I remember his self-imposed silence with the press and the grumbling it caused among the writers and television's talking heads. Now, in light of the big-mouthed stupidity of many of the NBA's boorish stars, his reticence is refreshing.

I remember a neighbor who was so caught up in the fever of the Sycamores' march toward the Final Four that he promptly went out and painted "Bird #33" on the yellow poplar slats of his graying barn in broad white letters. To the day that old barn fell to the wrecking ball, Bird's name endured with it.

I remember a night in Hulman Center when he allowed me to see what I think may be the greatest shot I ever saw. He slipped off a down screen to catch the ball on the wing, and as he drove to the baseline he was cut off by two trapping defenders. In mid-air, Bird switched the ball from his right hand to his left and calmly dropped a 10-footer through the nets. I can't recall now who said it and why, but a line I once heard seems apt for that seemingly effortless effort: "He showed no more emotion than last year's bird nest."

I remember the 49 he put up against Wichita State; I remember how much I hated Billy Packer; I remember Bird, with a pair of cheerleaders, grinning on the cover of Sports Illustrated; and I remember his guest appearances with "Captain Jack" on a local afternoon kids' show. I can still hear somebody singing a song about "Indiana having a new state bird."

I remember his no-look passes and graceful jumpers, but I also remember that he was, to speak euphemistically, very physical; some said he was dirty. Bird didn't just win because he was a gifted player; he won because he held a monopoly on the will to win. There was very little he wouldn't do to win, and I think that was the case whether he was playing in front of thousands or in a pick-up game on somebody's backyard concrete. Ask anyone who ever played against Larry Bird about what it was like, and I'd bet that they didn't feel finessed by him; they felt mugged by him, tormented by him, pick-pocketed by a country hick with street smarts.

I remember seeing him sitting with a towel over his head after the only loss of his senior year—that, of course, to Magic Johnson and Michigan State in the NCAA championship game. I thought he had been cheated out of something that was rightfully his. The fans had just gone along for the magnificent ride of a magical season; to me, there wasn't much to this "we won" stuff. He and his teammates were the ones who truly deserved to cut the nets that day, one last time.

I can still remember seeing him in Celtics green, with his two-ringed crew socks and his black All-Stars. I see him pick off that inbound pass and feed DJ to beat Detroit, and I see him out-duel Wilkins in perhaps the best quarter he ever played as a pro. I hear him dedicate a world championship to Terre Haute, see him smoke Red Auerbach's cigar, replay in my head the pass he threw at Bill Laimbeer's face.

I can see his head bounce off the floor in a game against the Pacers, see him on his belly along the sidelines trying to ease the pain of his ailing back. I see him run the pick-and-roll with Chief and open the back door with McHale. I see him work the refs, tangle with Dr. J, and shoot from behind the backboard, balanced near the end line like a giant ballerina. I can see him as if he were still playing in a Boston Garden that's no longer there, and I can still hear the shoveled gravel of Johnny Most's voice too.

When I think about Larry Bird, I wonder why there is no player at any level of the game today who truly reminds me of him, that there's no one who plays like he played, has the fire in him like he had. When I think of that, I'm both a little happy and a little sad.

On the day my son was born nearly 17 years ago, I promptly drove into town and bought him a pair of high-topped basketball shoes, a green and white basketball, and a Celtics T-shirt. I wanted my boy to grow up to love the game as much as I did, but I wanted him to someday play it like Bird, who by that time was battling, not only that traitorous back, but spurs in his heels and the certainty that he couldn't play the way he once did.

Almost from the time Bird's days in Terre Haute ended 25 years ago, we've moaned about what we lost when he left. Hoisting his uniform to the rafters Saturday will be a celebration of what we all still have by seeing him play.

When I think of Larry Bird, I know I was lucky to have seen the best.

Real men square bale and row boats
March 17, 2004

When Olympic hopeful Dan Beery thinks back on what helped him become one of the best rowers in the world, he reaches one rather unusual conclusion: He baled hay as a country kid near Oaktown, Indiana.

"One of the things that I've learned," the 28-year-old Knox County native recently said, "is there was a great deal of confidence and work ethic that was instilled in me as a young man. The difference between me and people who grew up in the city is that they have never spent entire weeks in an Indiana summer baling square bales and stacking them in a barn. Practices and physiological testing don't seem intimidating to a person who has grown up accustomed to that kind of work."

Work he does. Now toiling with the National Rowing Team in Chula Vista, California, Beery is one of the top perforrners at the Olympic Training Center. In just a matter of weeks, he'll find out if he's going to Athens this summer to go up against the best competition in the world.

Just how did a big, rangy kid—Beery stands 6 feet, 7 inches and weighs 220 pounds—from a small Indiana town end up being a nationally-recognized rower? It wasn't just his experience paddling canoes as a Boy Scout; it started, oddly enough, with Coach Howard Sharpe, whose legendary coaching career came to an end at the school near Bicknell.

"Coach Sharpe actually taught me post moves as a 7-year-old. He said that I was going to grow into a really big boy. He stressed the importance of fundamentals and of being able to run the fast break in my sleep, of knowing where my teammates would be on the floor, and being able to anticipate the movements of my teammates and opponents," Beery said.

Dan went on to play both football and basketball at North Knox, but in his junior season he suffered a neck injury that ended his football career, and by the middle of his senior year an ACL tear took away basketball for a while. He rehabilitated his knee and moved on to Bryan College in Dayton, Tennessee to play basketball, but left the small, liberal arts college for the University of Tennessee, Chattanooga two years later.

While playing in a pick-up game in the UTC sports complex, Beery was noticed by rowing coach, and former Olympian, Robert Espeseth, who just happened to be walking by. Espeseth invited Beery to practice with the rowing team on the nearby Tennessee River and soon realized that his hunch was going to pay big dividends.

"As a basketball player, I was not a great leaper or exceptionally quick, by any means; however, I did have the ability to push myself and work very hard,"

Beery says. "God has also blessed me with so many wonderful coaches. . . they've taught me the most important lessons, which are to be focused, work extremely hard, and be coachable or willing to learn about the game."

Beery learned all right, but it hasn't been easy. After winning the novice competition at the winter indoor rowing event, he went on to become UTC's team captain and most valuable rower. He spent summers in Philadelphia rowing for the prestigious Penn Athletic Club, competing for and winning several medals, including the gold in the US National Championships. Last summer, Beery was part of a pair-with-coxswain (two men rowing, one man directing them) that competed in Lucerne, Switzerland, then won a silver medal in Seville, Spain. He went on to compete in the British Royal Henley, then captured gold in Milan, Italy with his teammates.

"I hope that my rowing career means something special to people in my hometown. I want them to know that I was cut from my first national team camp. I lost trials for the national team in 1998, 1999 [twice], 2000, and 2001... To them, I hope it means never giving up."

If you're wondering if Dan Beery is too good to be true, if he really does revel in the hard work and sweat and pain, I suspect you're right. In rowing, Dan usually sets his sight on a finish line a few thousand yards of water ahead of him. It's interesting that he's reached so many other goals along the way.

It wasn't just tossing hay bales that taught perseverance to Beery; his mother, Merry, and dad, Jim, had a hand in that. "Personally, I believe I was raised in such a loving environment that I always believed in myself. I also knew that if I failed, that love and support would always be there. This is probably the biggest reason why I never gave up," Dan says.

A farmer friend of mine often wears a cap that reads, "Real men square bale." To me, there's at least another good man I know of who used to square bale. Now, he rows a boat.

******Author's Note: Dan Beery went on to capture Olympic Gold in Athens in the summer of 2004.***

The Best of the Basketball Stories...

Fourth Quarter
Fall 2004-Winter 2009

It's been a real rebuilding year
October 27, 2004

This is supposed to be a basketball column; I'll get to that in a while. I may not be writing about a team sport today, but this is, nonetheless, about a team.

Our contractor just called. The poor guy spent a good part of his summer working on my lopsided old place, and I know he thought he was done with it. He and a buddy tacked on a few new rooms, poured quite a bit of concrete, and remodeled our ugly garage.

Now, he's coming back one last time tomorrow to re-hang a door and work on a balky shower.

Despite the fact that he's moved on to other jobs, he thanked me, as always, before he hung up the phone. My wife and I have spent the better part of 20 years waiting for this building project to grow out of the sticky brown clay of our country hillside. Little did we know that the two men who drove the nails and finished the drywall would also teach us something: lessons worth as much or more than the wood and mortar in our new addition.

Kevin Milbourn and Rusty ("Rus-Dog," as my son came to call him) Thomas started our job from scratch in July. They pulled an old deck off the back of our house, tore away quite a bit of faded siding, popped out a decrepit backdoor, and then proceeded to dig a hole in my yard about the size of Hulman Center. They spent days slinging more dirt than even the candidates in the 8th Congressional District race can imagine, and when it rained, they had to double-lace their work boots for fear of losing them to the glue-like flypaper we call our soil.

I don't believe that I ever heard the pair utter a word about sports; the battered radio they sometimes listened to while they stuffed insulation in a ceiling or shimmed a window level, never played a ballgame; it wasn't set to the local sports show to help pass the hours they spent working in the steaming August heat. As a matter of fact, I didn't hear those two say much of anything; they worked in a fascinating, telepathic sort of way. When one needed a board, the other had it ready; when the other wanted a steady hand, the other was there kneeling nearby to lend it.

This team has worked together for so many years on so many kitchens, set so many rafters, and wired so many receptacles, that they move together like a well-choreographed team. Believe me, there has to be an unspoken trust between two men when one holds a two-by-four stake while the other pounds it into the rock-hard dirt of a sun-baked yard with a sledgehammer.

I did discover that as a kid, despite not weighing more than 135 pounds soaking wet, Kevin once aspired to play a little high school football. If there was a full-body cast made in heaven, I imagine it awaited him after practice. He told me that he eventually gave up the game, I imagine, just to save his parents the medical bills. I know he can play in pain though; he came to work the day after he fell off a ladder working on our job, and to my knowledge, Rusty never missed a minute of work either.

In their wake, I was as busy this summer as I have ever been. Even yet, a friend of mine and I are hustling to finish making my sassafras door and window trim in his cluttered woodshop. We also spent over three weeks of our evenings trying to beat the sunsets as we replaced that old deck with a newly expanded version. I've sown grass seed, re-built flower beds, and slathered enough stain and polyurethane on our doors and woodwork to put Bob Villa to shame. The labor has helped me appreciate all the more the people that I know who work with their backs and hands to scratch out a living.

Now, the sports application: There are too few times in sports these days that I can witness the kind of teamwork that Kevin and Rusty so easily share. It's not very often that I see friends working together toward a common goal. When I see that perfectly executed backdoor pass, the high five given to a player who dove to the floor after a loose ball, the coach who tells his players he's proud of their effort, or even the team standing on the sidelines in anticipation of a rarely used substitute getting off that one hopeful free throw, well, that's a Mozart concerto; it's a good book on a rainy day; it's a walk in the fresh fall air. It's like watching two men build something out of nothing.

So, what did I learn about sports from two guys who probably can't hit an open jumper to save their lives? Well, among other things, their partnership reminded me that a team, any team, needs a goal, that a team has to be ready for changes (we threw them a few), and that above all, hard work will pay off in the end, especially for teammates who are friends.

In the past few weeks, gyms have opened all across the Wabash Valley, and it's those kinds of lessons aspiring basketball players had better learn right along with reverse pivots and outlet passes.

One of my favorite home-spun philosophers is humorist Kin Hubbard. Years ago he said, "Nothing is as irritating as the fellow who chats pleasantly while he's overcharging you."

I used to spend a few minutes every day talking to Kevin and Rusty in the fading late afternoon light, nosing over what they'd accomplished. Overcharged? Not me. Guys, it was worth the money.

Now, when do we start on the kitchen?

Thanks, thanks a lot for...
November 25, 2004

Since this column comes out on Thanksgiving Day, I thought I'd take the time to sit down and write about some of the things for which I'm thankful. I'll not mention much about how fortunate I am to have a wonderful family and a warm home, or the fact that I hold a good job, have a couple of good buddies, and live in the fresh country air. After all, I'd be an idiot if I weren't already thankful for those things year round.

Of course, I'm paid to write about sports, so I'll narrow things down a bit without going into details as to why I'm also thankful for a plate of good fried chicken, the stacks of books I have in my office that I have yet to read, having a second bathroom, and that I can come home from work and put on my favorite pair of blue jeans. I'd better get going...

I'm thankful for the chance to walk into a high school gym about any night I want to and watch a game on just about any night of the week through March. I know it's not the pros, and most games are played by kids who struggle with trigonometry and making curfew, but I also know it's being played for the right reasons. It's nice knowing that kids rode to those games on school busses, that they're coached mostly by people who want them to be better people, not just better players, and that most of those kids will make friendships that will last them for the rest of their lives. There's something to be said about any game that can do that.

I'm thankful for athletic boosters, those tired and few who sell candy bars and dill pickles and nachos night after night to give our kids what they need, from uniforms to meal money. There are a lot of folks out there who are more than willing to sit and watch other people work; I think it's great that a handful get it done.

I'm thankful for my memories of what professional basketball used to be like, and yes, I do mean the game when it was played with less powerful, perhaps less athletic guys in short shorts and crew cuts. I'm happy to remember the days of good screens and complicated patterns, Elgin Baylor and Jerry West, John Havlicek and Bill Russell, Bobby Leonard and Mel Daniels. I got to know Billy Keller a little when I worked his basketball camp a few times years ago. He played for a reason that I suspect might seem foreign to a lot of current players now.

I'm thankful I got to see Larry Bird play basketball. I grew up worshipping the men who played on the radio as I tuned into the game in the dark of my bedroom. But I got to see Bird play just down the road and in person, and when someone asks me who the best player I ever saw was, I know I'll never have to hesitate with the answer.

I'm thankful for backyard rivalries. Those kinds of things may sound a bit archaic now, but if you don't understand what it's like to see two teams from schools that have long-standing traditions of wanting to beat one another, then get to the Banks of the Wabash Tournament at Rockville the first week of December or watch the North-South game. It's worth more than the four bucks you'll pay to get in, if you can find a seat.

I'm thankful for the people who have the thick skin and time to referee. I mean that. I know that when I coached I probably rode referees as much as anyone; I expected them to be perfect. Well, they're not perfect, but they are right most of the time, and they aren't blowing a whistle to get rich. Most do it because they love basketball. There really isn't any other reason.

I'm thankful that kids today don't have to wear the uniforms that players donned years ago. I mean wool warm-ups, satin shorts with belts, and skin-tight jerseys. For girls it was culottes and bobby sox. I hate the look of the too-long, baggy shorts that most players wear today, but at least they're comfortable.

I'm thankful for the Pizza Hut Classic. I look forward to it every December now, and I hope the players and coaches who are involved in it understand just how lucky they are. There's a generation of Valley players who fell through the cracks between the old Valley days and the PHWVC; it's been too long in coming, and we should thank the folks who make it happen.

I can't say I know why I thought of it just now, but I'm thankful for the basketball goal I had as a kid. It was a piece of plywood tacked onto a locust pole, but I loved it as if it were planted in Conseco Fieldhouse. I'm thankful that I've learned that starting out in life with the best of everything is a curse, not a blessing.

I'm thankful for cold milk and warm cookies and a good heater in my truck, for the fact that my kids don't have tattoos, and I've never been forced to watch

"Desperate Housewives," for regular mail, and morning coffee.

I'm thankful you're reading this.

Got long locks? You're hair today, cut from team tomorrow
December 7, 2004

No matter how hard I tried to convince her otherwise, my cousin's grandmother labeled me "a naked hippie" years ago. She'd often be sitting at my aunt's kitchen table when I blew through the backdoor looking to raid a refrigerator well stocked with popsicles and cold milk, and she'd look at me as if I were eyeing her purse.

I'll admit that I used to let my hair grow pretty long in those hot summer days, and since I was a country kid, I often went shirtless and shoeless too. But despite my penchant for sports and girls and baling hay, I don't think she was ever convinced that, as long as my hair covered my ears, I'd amount to much more than a considerable stretch at a state correctional facility.

Now, the shoe is on the other foot; my son gave our family stylist most of the past few months off, and it's been his kin, including me, who've been suggesting that he get his hair out of his eyes and off his collar. Most remember when he liked a crew cut, as straight as a board across the front and as flat as a pool table on top.

Then, just prior to the season starting, his basketball coach "asked" a few of his boys to get their hair trimmed and a few more to get used to the idea of shaving every couple of days. They didn't particularly like the request, but they did it, despite the pleas from girlfriends and classmates who thought the longer, scragglier dos and furry jaw lines were attractive.

My son's coach, Charlie Martin, asked me if, as a parent, I minded his anti-hirsute agenda, and I could only say that it was his prerogative. My son, a real student of history when he can use it in an argument, suggested that Pete Maravich had long hair, and he led the NCAA in scoring three times.

"Okay, when he scores 44 a game, he can let his hair grow," his coach said.

Do local high schools have policies that require players to have short, neatly groomed hair and whisker-less chins? Most coaches I spoke with said their schools have no written rules; it's the coach himself who calls the shots on the locks.

Northview's Mitch Lancaster puts it simply: "It's the coach's job to tell the kids about their hair. He has to be the judge and the jury. We don't allow sideburns below the ears, and we allow no facial hair. We preach doing things for the team. It's about team conformity."

By the way, Mitch isn't always a drill sergeant, and his Knights, like my son and his buddies, understand and do get their hair cut with a minimum of grumbling.

Rockville's Dave Mahurin—a tall, somewhat Shakespearean figure with his neatly trimmed Vandyke —makes it clear where the hair policy stands for his Rox.

"I ask my kids to have short hair and to be clean shaven," he says. "At my parents' rule meeting I further explain that 'short' hair is subjective. I also explain that the rule is a very good way to see who really wants to play. If having long hair is more important than playing basketball, then playing is not all that important."

Like Lancaster, Mahurin's approach to his players is all about team

"My rationale is that I want my kids to look similar to promote a team concept. We wear similar shoes, don't allow wrist bands or head bands, unless we all have them, and keep things as uniform as possible," he says.

He also thinks, like most coaches do, that the rules his kids learn to follow now, make them better men later. "Often times today kids feel the need to stand out or look different. That doesn't make them bad kids; however, it doesn't promote team unity either. Team sports offer the opportunity to be a part of a group of individuals working together as one. This is not in vogue or a trendy attitude in society today, but learning to sacrifice and develop self-discipline can be a great asset in an individual's life," the former Terre Haute South star said.

As for the Riverton Parke coach, Martin thinks that what kids are seeing on television influences what we're seeing at the high school level.

"I think that kids today just emulate what they see on TV with the NBA players. I think the NBA players do it to make themselves stand out as individuals, but at the high school level we're still more concerned with the team as a group rather than the individual. And, since my high school players do not make more money, yet, than I do [like NBA coaches], I still have some authority in their appearance. I'm not usually a big rules guy, but I am a big team guy. I felt that this [his hair policy] would be a way for our players to put their individuality second to the team," Martin says.

Martin may have another motivation: "As to facial hair, since I'm unable to grow a goatee, I am not going to be shown up by a bunch of teenagers," the well-shorn coach added.

The worst haircut I ever had was the one I performed as an eight-year-old on myself. I did so much damage in front of our bathroom mirror in just a few minutes that even my grandfather, known for notoriously bad haircuts as long as they were cheap, was a bit ashamed to take me to the barber. My mom took to hiding the scissors; folks at church just laughed.

Up until a few weeks ago, I found myself leaving every pair of clippers and snippers in the house in plain sight, hoping my son would take the hint and a whack at his own bangs.

Are hair policies old-fashioned, a bit tyrannical, a tad dictatorial? They sure are, and I love 'em.

Teammates to the very end
January 19, 2005

Jack Williams, Oscar Session, and Cliff Phillips remained teammates long past the now faded cheers they heard a half century ago. A coach and two players, they were men who first loved a game, then came to love one another as friends and brothers.

Jack died last month at age 86 after a long illness, but in the old days, he was a brash, well-dressed, and confident basketball coach at Glenn High School, a tiny, mostly rural institution on the eastern edge of Vigo County.

Oscar and Cliff were two of Williams' brightest stars. To most, the pair was just two more poor, black farm kids who had more dirt than dimes to their names. Most people may have believed that, but Jack didn't.

In the few years that Williams coached at Glenn, the trio came to know one another. Through the often brutal conditioning runs of up to four miles before their real practices even began, to the quiet car trips home that Jack offered the two exhausted boys to save them another five miles on foot, it seems mutual respect grew first, then came a deep and abiding friendship.

By 1951, Oscar and Cliff, and their talented teammates had help Jack build the pirates into the second-ranked team in Indiana. Within the next few years, Williams had quit coaching to become a school administrator. Oscar went on to graduate from Michigan State University and began a long career as a grade school principal. Cliff left Indiana State after a knee injury ended his basketball career and went to work at Alcan.

But somehow, through all the trials and tribulations that life threw at the three, they never lost touch, never lost sight of the friendship first forged by a game. Jack saw to it that Oscar stayed in college, and that Cliff had a job when Alcan closed its doors. Years before, the man who had made them run the lines and execute patterns to perfection, had also protested when local restaurants wouldn't allow his black players to eat in their dining rooms. He taught his players the social graces, taught them to stand up for themselves and to demand respect from an often-bigoted society.

One Glenn fan warned Williams that if he put even two black players together in his starting line-up, the home crowd would get up and walk out of the gymnasium. Jack responded by starting four black athletes, and within a month his school was renting a larger gym in Terre Haute to hold the overflowing Pirates' fans.

In the long run, it was Jack who needed Oscar and Cliff as much or more than they needed him. Controversy followed him as a coach: Oscar's brother, Charlie, generally regarded as one of the best players of his era, was ruled ineligible by the IHSAA after Glenn won its second consecutive Wabash Valley tournament title in 1951, and eventually that championship was forfeited.

Despite continued success after Charlie's graduation, Williams decided to quit coaching within just a few years and never returned to the sidelines. In the past few years, Jack and his wife, Marie, needed Oscar and Cliff even more. A series of strokes slowed Jack; Marie's passion for the piano and painting were hampered by macular degeneration.

The former players saw to it that Jack and Marie got to their doctor's appointments, that their mail was collected, that their home was maintained, and that their bills were paid on time. They were there to walk Jack to the car, to run Marie to the library, to go to the grocery store. Jack once told me, "They've been awfully good to us."

On a foggy December morning five years ago, my son and I met with the three old Pirates over breakfast to talk basketball. Through the steam of the hot coffee and the aroma of fried bacon, Oscar and Cliff sat across from "Coach" and wove their stories. All three ordered their "usual," and while we waited for our meals to arrive, folks around us giggled and smiled and shook their heads as they overheard the five of us gossip and laugh and talk about the old days.

In his gray fedora, black turtleneck, and camel hair sport coat, Oscar continued to wear the clothes of a man who was used to rising early to nattily meet the noise of children at the school door. He is a dignified and quiet man who laughs nearly under his breath. He may have spent much of his life in Michigan, but he came home and lived just a few doors away from Coach.

Cliff is more animated; he never meets a stranger. He is energetic and on that day wore an Indiana University jacket. The freckles on his broad nose spread wide atop the grin he permanently wears as he happily kids and chides and digs. He enthusiastically claims he'd still like to own a horse before he's 70.

We, of course, spoke of the glory days: those four-mile jogs; beating big rivals like Gerstmeyer; the 30-game winning streak; the bus trips to northern Indiana; Jack's dreaded curfew; and being denied the opportunity to eat with white teammates in a number of restaurants. One bit of advice that Williams always gave his players came up too, that being about the three things that players should avoid: "candy, cokes, and girls."

"We knew he was lying to us about the girls," Oscar said. "He was married, and we knew that Marie wasn't exactly his sister."

Sadly, that morning passed away too quickly; the few years since then have passed too. As we walked to our cars, I realized that it wasn't just the stories, or the food, or the joking that I had most enjoyed, it was the friendship.

Friendships must stand the test of time. I know two men, knew a third, who understood that friends will see you through when others think you're through. Teammates should be like that, and these three men were teammates to the end.

Author's Note: Cliff Phillips passed away in the winter of 2008. Marie Williams, now in her 90s, and Oscar Session, still live in Terre Haute.

How lucky can a guy get...
February 2, 2005

I was reminded again last week that I'm a lucky guy. The thought hit me as my wife and daughter and I cruised the smooth, straight pavement of U.S. 41 to Veedersburg, where my son and his basketball-playing buddies were to face the Mustangs at Fountain Central.

I didn't feel very well when I dragged myself home from work that Tuesday afternoon, and I wasn't exactly thrilled when I had to pull my no-less-tired bones off our living room couch about an hour later to get behind the wheel of our car.

But that feeling changed a few miles down the road.

As we headed out of our drive and into the cold north wind that so often blows across the fields near our house in January, I glanced to the west and saw one of those glorious winter sunsets that makes me glad that I'll never have enough money to retire to Florida. I know, the sun goes down in that state, too, but I've always felt that somehow when I've had the privilege of seeing the sun dip below the frozen horizon of an Indiana cornfield, and the reds and pinks and oranges of the dusk fade into an inky darkness, well, I've lived a little. That was the case as we raced the sunset north.

There was no caravan of fans to join as we left Parke County and headed across the line into Fountain, no painted fan bus laden with rabid supporters for our team. For most part, we traveled the road alone, glancing over our right shoulders to see the stars and moon make their appearance, over our left to watch the last glimpses of the day die in something a little better than Technicolor.

As we hustled our way across the frozen tundra of Fountain Central's parking lot to the warm gym, the familiar scent of popcorn greeted us at the door. It felt good to hear the sounds of a B-team game: the cheers of the sparse crowd that had braved the cold; the chatter of friends and parents and students; the familiar squeal of sharp cuts and quick pivots on the glossy floor; the scream of an official's whistle.

Things went well for our boys that night, and after a 20-point win, a bag of that hot popcorn, and a post-game chat with an old coaching rival, who just happened to remind me of the time we once stood nose-to-nose at mid-court in that very gym questioning each others' integrity, the three of us piled back into a cold car to follow the taillights of other players' parents back home. The stars we saw on that night-time drive under a cloudless crystal sky just added a finishing touch.

Just before I sat down Saturday to begin writing this story, I went for a long walk in the snow along our country road, the sun nowhere in sight through the cold gray mist. As I walked into the frigid wind, the snow fell lightly on my shoulders and the breeze bit my face as I hunkered down into my barn coat and turned my eyes toward the ground until I could walk away from the breeze.

It was the night of our homecoming game, and within a few hours I would see my son, looking a little too serious, as he escorted a pretty girl onto the basketball floor as a junior attendant. After that, we watched his team tackle the talented South Putnam Eagles, and through the evening I ran into a dozen or so former students who used to call me "Mr." and a few more who once called me "Coach."

That evening, I sat in the bleachers soaking in the feel of the noisy gym and talked to two friends who had seen their boy play his last high school basketball game nearly 20 years ago.

"It goes by so quickly," they both said at nearly the same time. I didn't need the reminder.

There I was again, lucky.

Joseph's amazing Technicolor dream coats
February 16, 2005

Before you think I'm going into that old stand-up routine where the cigar-smoking comedian reminds his audience rather ungrammatically that, "You can call me Ray, or you can call me Jay, or you can call me R.J., but you doesn't has to calls me Johnson," I'll tell you that although my name is Mike, or Michael, my wife and mom have always called me Joe or Joseph, my middle name.

One of my best friends is also named Joe, and I recall a time when someone saw a note I had written to my wife—I added a few endearments—and signed it with that name. When that someone told Joe's wife, my buddy had a little explaining to do.

Anyway, I'm also a Joseph, and this story is about a pair of coveted coats I received this winter, ironically, about nine days apart. Actually, the whole thing is a little weird.

Anyone who knows me also knows that I love "Hoosiers," the classic film about a miracle high school basketball team called the Hickory Huskers that overcomes the odds and the damaged past of its resurrected coach to win the Indiana state championship in 1952. If you've seen the film, then you know that those mythical Huskers also wore letter jackets, or what is now called "authentic athletic apparel."

About two years ago, I saw a guy wearing a replica Huskers coat at the Wabash Valley Pizza Hut Classic, and I immediately began salivating for one. Last year, I realized that the lucky jacket wearer was Leigh Evans, who just happens to be, if it's possible, a greater fan of the movie than I am; he has the crew cut to prove it. If you don't already know, Leigh also runs one of the better basketball Web sites this side of hoops heaven, *HickoryHusker.com.*

When I saw Leigh at the Classic draw at Terre Haute South last November, I asked him if he knew where I could get a Huskers jacket, and I couldn't have imagined his response: "Sure. But if you wear an extra-large, I have one in my trunk. Do you want it?"

Now, Mrs. Lunsford had no stupid children, so I rarely look gift horses in the mouth. Ten minutes later, I was walking out of the Braves' gym proudly wearing the red and gold of Hickory High. I practically expected Jimmy and Ollie and the rest of the boys to meet me in the parking lot so we could run over to the park and shoot around before supper.

OK, now the weird part.

A little more than a week later, a week I had filled by proudly informing virtually everyone I knew how I got my new jacket and that I was contemplating Leigh's nomination for sainthood, I was called down to our school's main office by Assistant Principal Craig Newby. When I got there, Craig told me that I had a Christmas gift sitting on the school secretary's desk. He was right, but since Craig was encouraging me to rip it open and show everyone what I had, and since Craig and I have been known to pull a few gags at each others' expense, I decided to take the box back to my room. That way, if it exploded, contained embarrassing undergarments, or was in some other way a set-up, there'd be no witnesses.

Miraculously, the box contained a Hickory Huskers letter jacket and a note.

I first suspected that Craig had called my wife, had her hand over my jacket, then rewrapped it for me: the ultimate re-gifting scam. But he hadn't, and the tag dangling from the left sleeve convinced me it was a second new jacket.

The note and the coat came from an old high school friend, Steve Morris, a great referee, but an even better man. Steve had purchased a number of the jackets in Indianapolis and was handing them out like Basketball Santa to his refereeing buddies. He said that soon after he read one of my more nostalgic columns, he knew I needed to belong to what he called the "Hickory Husker Old School Letter Jacket Club." I am truly honored.

Before I wrap this story up, I have to tell you about another subplot that soon developed. Two of my closest pals, the real Joe (Joe Huxford), and Sam Ball, (a.k.a Steve Bell), saw my jacket[s], and each wanted one for himself. I'm no Solomon, who decided to cut the remaining jacket in two, so I thought I'd pass along Steve Morris' kindness and buy them each one. I tried for weeks to find them one, but by Christmas both had already told their wives, and on Christmas morning they had their own coats under their trees.

Not long ago, someone saw all three of us in our jackets. "You look like the three musketeers," he said. I don't care if we look like the Scarlet Pimpernels, I love the jackets, and the extra one will go to my son.

More importantly, Virginia, I believe in Santa Claus even more than I used to. I know that one of his helpers always carries a laptop computer with him; the other wears a striped shirt and blows a whistle.

Thanks guys.

It's time to read 'Play and learn and pass it on'
March 2, 2005

If you haven't read it already, my advice to you is to someday soon pick up one of the wisest little books I have ever read: H. Jackson Brown's "Live and Learn and Pass It On." Published in 1991, the slim little volume came on the heels of another big-time best seller, Brown's "Life's Little Instruction Book."

Both books are easy reading, simple lists of life lessons that either Brown compiled himself or recorded after asking people, ages "5 to 95," to simply tell him something that living a life has taught them.

It's a theory of mine that my students don't often talk with many folks outside their own age group, and since I liked the books so much, I decided to turn Brown's idea into an English class assignment, then into today's story.

With apologies to Brown, all I did was ask friends, students, current and former coaches, referees, managers, players from years gone by and years to come, guys and gals, oldsters and youngsters, to answer one question: "What has basketball taught you?"

The number of responses I've received is so great that I couldn't include them all today. I haven't gotten answers from anyone younger than 11 nor older than 60 this time around, but just give me a little more time. What I did include, in what I suspect will be just a first installment, are the gems that follow:

"I've learned that it's okay to be a 20/20 man; 20 seconds to go and 20 points ahead was my time to shine." Age 48

"I've learned that my lifelong and closest friends are the guys I grew up playing basketball with." Age 28

"I've learned that professional player does not mean professional person." Age 26

"I've learned that post players are only as good as their point guards." Age 39

"I've learned that a team that consistently wins is made up of more than one player." Age 17

"I've learned that basketball is like my relationship with my parents: the older I get, the more I appreciate them. It seems like when you're younger, you take them both for granted." Age 26

"I've learned that I'd rather sit on the bench than in the bleachers." Age 48

"I've learned that as much as I love basketball, there are more important things in life, but not many." Age 28

"I've learned that I don't always win." Age 11

"I've learned that getting a D on your report card won't kill you. That's what I got in gym class basketball." Age 46

"I've learned that during my elementary and junior high days I dreamed of being a basketball player. In high school and college I was fortunate to live my dream. Now, my enjoyment comes from watching others as they work hard to make their dreams come true." Age 60

"I've learned that you play for the name on the front of the jersey, and you are responsible for the name on the back of the jersey." Age 24

"I've learned that both basketball and life are marathons, not sprints." Age 36

"I've learned that I do a better job of officiating than I ever did playing." Age 46

"I've learned that basketball is about teamwork and winning, not about how many points you've scored." Age 18

"I've learned that if you fall down seven times, you have to get up eight." Age 37

"I've learned that I have more fun when I play with unselfish players." Age 30

"I've learned to keep my head up and to not take my eyes off the goal." Age 39

"I've learned that some of the best people I have ever known, even though many I hardly ever see anymore, were people I met through basketball." Age 46

"I've learned that satisfaction or approval from my coach was not based on the score at the end of game or the record at the end of the season, but by the effort put forth to get there." Age 28

"I've learned that I performed better when I didn't play to the crowd." Age 45

"I've learned that it's harder to coach the game than it was to play it." Age 29

"I've learned to make three in a row before you go." Age 56

"I've learned that the best coaches teach you about life and say they are just teaching you about basketball." Age 28

"I've learned that sitting on the bench makes you the best player on the team. Without you, the A players wouldn't be ready for the game." Age 17

Finally, I've learned by writing this column that finding wisdom isn't all that hard. I don't think there will ever be a need to scale a mountain to seek great knowledge.

All I have to do is simply ask a few friends.

She never cut down any nets, but she was a champion March 16, 2005

When I sat down to write today, I didn't know if I could finish a sentence. My mom passed away Sunday morning, and it's been tough for me, tough for my family.

Let me tell you about my mom. She was a worker and a worrier, a cleaner and a fixer; she was a good friend and faithful to many. Sports, one of the central threads that has wound its way through the lives of many in her family, wasn't very high on her list of priorities. On those lazy Sunday afternoons when we all congregated in Mom's cramped kitchen and spilled over into the living room with plates of fried chicken and mashed potatoes, we'd always have some sort of game on the television, and all she would say was, "Just keep it turned down."

My mom never had much time for games; I think she just thought they weren't that important and that people fretted too much over them. Near the end, she spent much of her day watching the TV from some sort of hospital or rehabilitation center bed, but it was almost certainly "Animal Planet" she had tuned in, not ESPN. I think that in a way she saw herself as one of those homeless cats or sick puppies the show features because after her stroke and heart attack, and a half-dozen surgeries, she found herself ricocheting between my sister's house, her own apartment, and an endless stream of waiting rooms, doctors' offices, rehab bicycles, and intensive care units.

We live in a day and age where a lot of people live and die by sports. Their day is made or ruined by the outcome of a game, a make or a miss, hoisting a championship trophy or hitting the showers early. Games are supposed to show us courage and grit and guts. I saw all those things in my mom's determination to get better, and in her eventual realization that she wasn't going to. She showed me those qualities more than any athlete I ever watched or coached or wrote about.

In her best days, I think Mom could have been a pretty fair athlete herself. She was tall and strong and kind of graceful. But over the years, she chose to devote her time to helping others, not competing with them. I never saw her throw a ball of any kind, not once, but she could make a quilt from a few scraps of cloth, bake a pie from scratch, spank her kid if he needed it, and move a couch with the best of 'em.

She canned whatever came from the garden, mended pants that other folks threw away, studied her Bible, read novels about the American West, wrote letters, cooked endlessly, cleaned her house, and visited friends who needed a hand, a listening ear, or one of the last dollars she had in her purse.

I grew up in a wonderfully warm house, in a wonderfully simple place, but in the past three hard years, I learned more about my mom than at any other time in our lives. She never put on the gloves, but she was a fighter; she never cut down any nets, but she was a champion; she never carried the load for any team or sought any glory, but she did quietly labor to care for others. Instead of threading the needle with a pass, she simply threaded a needle and went to work.

For some reason, she never felt as though she had done enough for us. One day, just a few weeks ago, my brother, John, and I were in her room as she finished her supper from a wheelchair. My tireless sister and brother-in-law were to be there soon to visit, and we found ourselves talking about the days when we were kids and the fun we'd had. I told Mom that I wouldn't have traded my childhood for anything, despite the fact that we never really had the money to do much. She cried a little and said she wished she had been able to give us more. Imagine that.

One of the last clear things I heard my mom say came in response to a nurse who had quietly slipped into her last hospital room to take her blood pressure. As the nurse slipped the cuff off Mom's arm, the nurse said

"Thank you," and Mom clearly responded with, "You're welcome."

That was Mom. She was polite, and she was kind. She knew the nurse was just doing her job.

Mom, you did your job, too. Thank you.

******Author's Note: This story ran on the day of my mother's funeral and the editors of the Tribune-Star decided to run it on Page 1; my new column, The Off Season, was born.***

It's time to seize the day, boys
November 14, 2005

One of my favorite movie scenes is in "The Dead Poets Society." In it, an innovative English teacher, John Keating, played by Robin Williams, leads his class of teenaged prep schoolboys to the school's trophy case. Behind the glass are the sepia-toned faces of ages-gone athletes, who, like the boys in that class, were once young and optimistic, with their lives in front of them.

I was reminded of that spot in the film the other day as I thumbed through an old notebook I keep for this column. Among the late-night ideas hastily scribbled on the note pads I leave by my bed, old game programs, and the letters I've kept from readers over the years, are a half-dozen photos from yellowed newspapers, now laminated in plastic to keep them from falling apart.

Two of the pictures are reprints from local papers of two of the best basketball teams in the history of the Wabash Valley. In another, I see myself standing beside a team that had just won the Parke County Tournament championship 21 years ago. It hardly seems possible that so much time has passed.

One of the other photos is of the 1932 Rosedale Hotshots, also the Parke County champions, although it was perhaps even more impressive than my team's feat: there were at least 11 schools in the county in those days. It was the same team that finished its 1933 season as runner-up to Hutsonville in the Wabash Valley Tournament; there were 94 schools entered to vie for the crown that year.

I knew a few of the men who played on that team: Herman Huxford, for one, passed away just a few years ago. The smile on his face suggests that, for once, he didn't have a chaw of tobacco in his mouth, but the Herman I knew is there anyway, tucked away behind a younger, less care-worn face. Another member of that squad, Everett Newton, still lives two miles down the road from my house.

The faces in that picture of Mudderbill McCurdy and Buck Bostick holding the championship trophy, of Glen Hartman and Coach Red Garrigus and the others, remind me that time marches on. It was another photo in my morning newspaper that reminded me even more of that just the other day.

Howard Mathas' obituary caught me a bit by surprise last week. Although he was 87, and I had not seen him for a few years, it always seems to surprise me when I see that someone who seemed indestructible has passed. Mathas coached basketball at a half-dozen Valley schools, including Rosedale, Glenn, and Wiley, winning a sectional tournament for the Red Streaks.

More than once I asked Howard if I could do a column about him, and he always declined, saying that surely I could find someone else who deserved it more. I doubt that; Howard was a nice man, a war hero, a fine coach, and a gentleman.

"He was just for the kids," says Jim Chaney, who played for Mathas at Rosedale toward the end of Mathas' tenure there as coach from 1947-1951.

"With Coach Mathas you always got the fundamentals. He was just a down-to-earth coach, and I mean to tell you, when he told you to do something, you did it," Chaney added.

In fact, Chaney and his classmates risked quite a bit to keep Mathas at Rosedale. When the coach was unceremoniously asked to leave as the Hotshots coach, Chaney and about 40 other students walked out of class in protest and promptly began to get signatures from townsfolk to keep their coach.

"It didn't do much good," Chaney said, "but he [Mathas] went on to Glenn and then Wiley, and he was very successful there."

The fact that Mathas was a special person was reinforced just a few days ago. I received a letter from Parker Eaton, another Rosedale grad, who, like Chaney, revered Mathas. "He was a coach that you would love to have your son play for," Eaton said.

He also told me that when he learned of Mathas' death, he called Harry Jukes, one of the best players to ever take the hardwood in Rosedale. Jukes lives in southern Louisiana but drove straight through to Indiana to attend his coach's funeral.

Ironically, one of the other old photos I had in that notebook of mine was of the 1936 Montezuma Aztecs. There on the front row sits number 3, Howard Mathas. His team won its first 10 games that season, many of them played in the old "Cracker Barrel," a tiny box of a gym built in 1928. In that photo, like the ones that Keating showed to his boys in the film, young men like Mathas, and his teammates, boys with names like Sherrill and Rohr and Marshall and Reel, still had their whole lives in front of them.

One of the things that Chaney told me just before we ended our phone conversation stayed with me a while.

"I think that just about everybody who ever played will tell you that he wishes he'd played harder or given it more than what he did. If you don't do that when you can, you'll regret it, sometimes for the rest of your life."

In a memorable scene, Keating reminds his boys to live the old adage, *carpe diem*: "seize the day." Howard Mathas must have believed that too.

Finding new life for an old place
April 4, 2006

Leo Maesch stood at half court of the old Clinton High School gymnasium a few Saturdays ago and told me why he's one of the folks who've worked so hard to keep the heat on, the doors open, and the kids playing on its floor. "I'm old, so I guess I like old things," he said.

Maesch, nearly 60, isn't as old as the building. Built, at least in part as a Works Progress Administration (WPA) project in 1936, the gym stayed open for business even after the high school relocated to a new spot across Highway 63 in 1978. After serving as a middle school until 1995, neglect caught up to the once sacred place, that is until it was purchased by the Allied Service Group in 2002 to use as an industrial training facility.

The company put thousands of dollars into preserving the building that housed the school's gymnasium and industrial arts and music rooms, but eventually Allied had to give up the facility altogether. That's when the Community Recreation Center, the building's new name, was born.

Maesch was quick to point out that he's no solo act. Clinton residents Brian McLeish (the CRC'S president), Bob Burkett, Doug Wilson, Greg Luce, D.J. Bonomo, Gary and LueAnne Andis, and Hugh and Donna McLeish, have put in countless hours at the CRC. For instance, the Andises methodically removed every bleacher in the gym, section by section, refinished them, and put them back—a true labor of love when you consider the five-gallon buckets of chewing gum they scraped from the undersides of the old seats.

That work has paid dividends: the gym is a very busy place these days. St. Mary-of-the-Woods uses the facility for its practices and all home games (what Brian McLeish calls a very positive partnership), South Vermillion's Wildcats hosted a number of boys and girls varsity games there, and everything from ISTEP tutoring to class reunions to the Business Women's Professional Club meetings has taken place on the premises.

"I would like to believe the CRC gym will have a positive impact on the entire community, not only in giving kids from Vermillion, Parke, Vigo, and Edgar Counties a place to play basketball, but also to offer so many more things to people of all ages. We see this as a center that will offer programs to benefit all those who live in our community," McLeish said.

McLeish, 40, who says he "loves to work with kids and watch them succeed," made the original contact with Allied about using the gym. "I attended Sacred Heart during my middle school years, so I only played in the gym when we played the SVMS team, and then during basketball camp in the summer," he added. A 1983 grad of South Vermillion, McLeish has eight aunts and uncles who all graduated from Clinton and shared stories with him about the gym.

Another Clinton resident who remembers the gymnasium well is 1970 grad, Mike Smith. Smith, 53, managed Rosenblatts' Department Store on Main Street in Clinton for 30 years, but remembers his time in the gym like it was yesterday. Ray Goddard was his coach for a while.

"At the time, I thought that all Coach Goddard taught us was basketball, but years later I realized I gained more knowledge about life and hard work than basketball," Smith says.

He recalled a night when Goddard's Wildcats faced Howard Sharpe's Gerstmeyer Black Cats in the old gym, and Lou Rendaci, who worked at the local Dodge dealership, installed seat belts on the benches for both coaches.

Smith said, "A home game was a special event. The gym was packed with fans, the student body, the cheer club, the band—which stayed the whole game—and coquettes and majorettes. Everyone just seemed to have a better sense of community spirit during those years."

"My most precious memory of playing ball in that gym is that while a game was being held, there would be a voice loudly saying my name from the crowd. That voice was my mom's, Bev Smith, someone who truly loved Clinton basketball. For myself, my brother, and my cousins, it seemed that no greater joy existed for her than attending a game in support of us," Smith added.

Smith's wife, Kathy, was a cheerleader, band member, and majorette at Clinton. She said, "My best memories of school are the times I spent in the gym. It seemed like the school revolved around the gym. The band made the place shake, and no one complained about having to go to the games. It was what we looked forward to all week."

Though McLeish and his CRC staff are very pleased with community support over its first eight months, they know it's going to take considerably more money to keep going. They've received great support from local businesses, the City of Clinton, and numerous individual volunteers. Grants from the Vermillion County Foundation, Eli Lilly, and the Clinton Lions Club have provided "seed money." He also says the CRC has a great working relationship with the South Vermillion Athletic Department, but it needs more.

"Like any not-for-profit organization, we rely on volunteers and the generosity of individuals and businesses," McLeish says. "It warms my heart to hear Clinton School alumni talk about playing, cheering, and just having fun in the gymnasium again."

If you happen to see Leo Maesch, remind him that he may think he's old, but at least in Clinton he lives in a community that likes to keep old things around a while longer than most.

It's not what we've gained, but what we've lost
November 30, 2006

I haven't seen much basketball this fall; the weather outside has been too nice lately to turn my attention to things indoors just yet. I hope the old adage of it being better late than never still rings true.

The idea for this story arrived on my front step soon after I received a call from a faithful reader, Judy Hughes. Judy had taken in an old Rosedale High School yearbook from her friend, Margaret Beauchamp Rambacher. Margaret's brother, Dick, found the book in their father's [Harry Beauchamp] belongings, and Harry's kids just wanted to see the old annual displayed somewhere, perhaps at the school.

I do mean it's old too; it's a 1922 "Outlook," the very first of its kind.

Judy knew that I'd fawn over the thing like the Holy Grail. Its cover is a crumbling green construction paper, and it had been kept in plastic before she ever gave it to me. Like any curator who has been loaned an antiquity from a rival museum, it's going to truly take willpower for me to give the book up to someone else. The annual has certainly given me a look at the past, though—one of the primary reasons we have yearbooks to begin with—but it's also given me a glimpse at our future too.

Many of the names in The Outlook can still be found attached to some of the good folks who live in my end of the county. But above all, the yearbook has shown me not how much we've gained in the last 80 years or so, but rather how much we've lost.

There's not an abundance of photos in the annual, but those that are there mostly show a generation, that for some reason, appears more serious, more determined about tackling life than mine did. Virtually all of The Outlook's illustrations were hand drawn, and the seven-member faculty that was pictured, including principal Lee Owens, who also taught history and Latin, was young, starch-collared, and well-groomed.

English teacher Ellen Newkirk appeared kind and intelligent; writing teacher Roy Williams parted his hair down the middle and had a humorous smile on his face. The advertisements in the back of the book allowed me to see just how vibrant and active the now-sleepy little town of today once was with its lumberyard and car dealership, its meat market and restaurants, its barber shop and hardware store. It really was a different world in those days when the trains stopped at every little burg on the line, and kids kicked coal off the cars to help heat their homes.

There were apparently only two sports offered to Rosedale athletes in 1922, both coached by a baby-faced physical education teacher named Clyde Cunningham. There were no girls' teams. The baseball season was played over three weeks in the fall; there were 10 boys on the team, and they won four of their five games, the last played on Oct. 24, an 8-2 win over Fontanet, just 10 days after the Beantowners had defeated the Rosedale squad 8-6.

Basketball must have started on the heels of baseball; it was obviously the sport of choice since the 10 players on the roster and Coach Cunningham enjoyed a 20-game schedule and more space was devoted to it in the yearbook.

I'm not sure that the school had an official nickname for its teams yet; there isn't one to be found in the annual. I do know that Rosedale teams were calling themselves the Hotshots by 1930 or so. At one time the teams called themselves the Colts.

Rosedale's biggest blowout in the 1921-22 season was a 35-2 win over county-rival Bridgeton; the squad then dropped a 34-10 decision at Marshall, another Parke County team, in its biggest loss a few days later. Long, and I'm sure, cold, road trips included travels to Concannon, Farmersburg, and Bellmore.

I also noticed that all of the players on the team had nicknames. We don't do that much anymore. I have no way of knowing why Harry Jukes was nicknamed "Boola," why team captain Eli Seville was called "Skee" either. Donald "Pickle" Reeves and Eugene "Red" Taylor were on that roster too.

On one of the opening pages of The Outlook is a picture of the school as it stood in 1922. It's hard to imagine that the building sat in what is now the town park, a stone's throw from Main Street. The players who were returning for the 1922-23 season were promised a new gymnasium by the school board; they actually played in a tiny room above the old diner in town for a while, avoiding beams that supported the roof and bouncing the ball off the ceiling into the basket.

As much of a basketball fanatic as I am, I have to admit that my favorite section in The Outlook is the one where the senior pictures sit next to the lists of the soon-to-be-graduates' school activities; their own personal mottos were included. How sincere they looked, how serious those 13 seemed to be.

Basketball player Herm Walters' motto was "Dare to do your duty always; this is the height of true valor." Boola Jukes' read: "Before us lies the timber; let us build." Class president Elizabeth Conley's was, "Keep true to the dreams of thy youth."

Glenn Cowger, who played basketball for three years, acted in the class play, and who helped put the yearbook together, chose this motto: "I desire no future that will break the ties of the past."

I couldn't agree with him more.

Winners in every sense of the word
November 27, 2007

Clyde Lovellette, Greg Bell, and Terry Dischinger have a lot in common. They were born in Terre Haute, attended Garfield High School within a few years of one another, and shared the thrill of their lives by bringing home gold medals from three different Olympic Games. But I think all three men share something else that is perhaps even more rare these days than the awards and accolades that came their way in Helsinki and Melbourne and Rome: dignity and humility.

Like nearly 200 other people, I listened to this trio of winners at the "Breakfast With The Champions" on November 17 at the Holiday Inn in Terre Haute. In a gesture of appreciation for the accomplishments of these men, Gary Fears and Brian Miller and a handful of other local businessmen and city officials, took it upon themselves to find a way to do an impressive makeover on a little patch of turf in Twelve Points and rename it The Gold Medal Plaza. In doing so, it was their hope, as Mayor Kevin Burke put it in his remarks, "that our young people can know of this, and that they would want to live up to these men."

"Had ESPN been around in the 1950s, Terre Haute would have been recognized as a breeding ground for greatness," Fears said in realization that Lovellette and Dischinger grew up in the same city block, and that Big Clyde and Bell attended a number of the same classes together.

The medalists have grown to become great friends over the years, something not lost on Dischinger when he said that when they had all been chosen to be honored elsewhere, he was not going to be able to attend. Lovellette and Bell said that if that was the case, they wouldn't go either; they would wait until all three could appear together.

Lovellette's accomplishments are legendary. An all-state center who took his Purple Eagles to the championship game of the Indiana state tournament in 1947, he became a dominant player who led the University of Kansas to the national championship in 1952. He then became the man in the middle for the Minneapolis Lakers, as well as other professional teams, but not before he beaded to the Olympic Games to earn the Gold. Known as a fierce competitor, Lovellette said, "I really am a nice guy. I just always wasn't [nice] on the floor."

Now living in the snowy regions of the upper peninsula of Michigan, Lovellette said, "I'll never forgot Terre Haute or Garfield or the coaches I had. It's always great to be back here, but I felt years ago that there was some resentment that I never attended Indiana or Purdue or Indiana State." He went on to say that the mere fact that his college coach, the great Phog Allen, had learned the game from its inventor, Dr. James Naismith, and that Allen had promised him a national championship, was enough to convince him to become a Jay-hawk.

In tears during his acceptance speech, Lovellette simply said, "Thanks" as he headed back to his seat, and I soon came to understand that Clyde Lovellette is a big man in more than one way.

Bell, the winner of the long jump competition at the Games in Melbourne in 1956, made it very clear that although he had won a Gold medal, he understood that it would not be a "free pass" in life. Fiercely competitive as well, he knew what it was like to sit in the back of the bus. "But now," he said, "life is a long journey, and it's from the back of the bus to the front table." He went on to say about the experience of standing on the winner's platform at the Olympics, "My cynic's heart skipped a beat, and there was a lump in my throat."

A prominent dentist now living in Logansport, Bell said, "I thank God that He has blessed me, and I hope to never stop learning. I want to thank the people whose hands touched my life.

"Some people die between their ears," he told the audience, but that hardly applies to Bell himself. A successful poet, he closed his comments by reciting one of his own poems, "I Believe in You." Undoubtedly thinking of local physician William Bannon, who played an important role in shaping the athlete's life, Bell said, "...And you know you owe the thanks for these dreams of yours come true/To the faith of all the people who said, 'I believe in you.'"

Greg Bell may have been rightfully indignant; now, he's simply a wise man.

Dischinger, now living in Portland, Oregon, said that he was "privileged to grow up in this town." "Disch" has led a fascinating professional life, both in and out of sports, but appears to be well grounded in what matters most to him. "I want to thank my mom and dad for raising me with the idea that what comes first in life is your relationship with God," he said as he opened his comments.

The case has been made that Dischinger may be the greatest all-around athlete to ever come out of Vigo County, but despite being on a world championship Babe Ruth baseball team, being an outstanding football and track star, and a great all-around basketball player at Purdue University and in the NBA—besides winning the Gold—Dischinger spent most of his time at the podium reminiscing about his days in the north end of the city. He fondly remembered playing touch football at Collett Park, spending his bus fare on doughnuts and walking home after swimming at the YMCA, going to the movies at the old North drive-in, taking part in yo-yo contests, and sitting at the soda fountain at West's drugstore.

He recalled the hours he spent playing baseball at Spencer Field, shopping at the department stores downtown, and the tremendous rivalries his Garfield teams had with Gerstmeyer and Wiley. "I had a special place to live in as I grew up," he said.

Like Lovellette and Bell, Dischinger grew emotional as he spoke of accepting his medal in Rome. "It was a surreal experience," he said before returning to the subject of his coaches and friends and family in the mellow and relaxed voice of a happy man.

Before Fears closed the program, he said, "It's been an incredible experience to associate with such wonderful human beings. The people of Terre Haute are better for knowing the likes of these three fine gentlemen-athletes."

He took the words right out of my mouth.

Thumbing through a real history book
January 16, 2009

My wife and I invest a bit of our time on the occasional Saturday wandering through antique stores and junk shops. We do more picking up and putting down than shelling out and loading up, but I was convinced that I couldn't have made a better investment last fall than when I laid down $7.00 for a history book; at least it's a history book to me.

It's a "J.C. Higgins Official College Basket Ball Score Book," a 5"x8" glance at the past made expressively by Sears and Roebuck & Co. of Chicago, and it was purchased and used for the 1924-25 high school basketball season by tiny Judyville High School.

I kept a scorebook for two local schools years ago, and I enjoyed my time at the scorer's table. It's the best seat in the house, and there's a sense of accomplishment that comes from keeping an accurate and orderly scorebook or getting a thumbs-up from two appreciative game officials or a slap on the back from a coach who is happier with your neat columns of 2's and completely filled 0's than he is with his team.

Judyville's coach was, in all probability, more pleased with his scorekeeper, one Francis Regan, than his team in the winter of '24-'25. His squad, most likely called "cagers" since they weren't too far removed from the era when a wire cage occasionally enclosed the playing floor, went just 2-5, and one of those victories came by forfeit.

Like so many whistlestops from the glory days of Indiana small towns, Judyville still exists today, but more in theory than reality. Tucked away in Warren County's Liberty Township, the burg actually grew because founder John Finney Judy (originally spelled Tschudi) owned a prosperous farm. Founded in 1903, the town eventually had its own telephone company and, according to an Internet encyclopedia entry, actually minted a "local form of currency known as 'Judy Money,'" which was accepted throughout the county. Judyville grew as it gained both a trunk line of the old Eastern Illinois Railroad and a post office.

I couldn't find much of anything about the school there, but the proof that one existed, and that it had a basketball "five" came in the form of that yellowing scorebook that I picked up nearly 85 years after the fact. I'm pretty certain that Judyville High never won a sectional; I have no idea what the team nickname was.

The scorebook is an open window on old, old school Indiana basketball. Since the book never lists a game being played at Judyville, it is probable that the school had no gym, an obstacle that many Indiana schools faced in those days. The first game recorded in the book came on October 10, 1924: the Judyville team facing Ambia's Wildcats at Ambia and losing 46-12. Regan listed the five Judyville players by positions, referring to them as right and left forwards, a center, and a back and front guard. Only one referee was used, Glen Farrel.

County rival Williamsport followed four days later. The Bombers apparently lived up to their nickname, handing Judyville a 54-4 loss; Williamsport's Robert King scored 24 points, while all of Judyville's points came on free throws: two in each half.

On Nov. 1, Judyville traveled north to Boswell in southern Benton County and picked up its first victory of the year despite playing no game; the Blackhawks couldn't field a team, and Judyville was declared a 2-0 winner. Six days later, it was back to Ambia and another loss, 35-15, despite the fact that two more names appeared in the scorebook for Judyville.

It took a little over a month before Regan made another entry for a game, and it involved a first team from Judyville defeating a second team, 27-19; the additional players Judyville had picked up in the interim apparently made no difference. Three days later they faced the Bombers at Williamsport again, and this time the host school showed no mercy in crushing them 98-10.

The second Williamsport game and its score was much more common to old-time Indiana hoops than is often believed. Most of the individual and team scoring records in the books in this state come from the earliest era of our basketball heritage. For instance, Judyville's old nemesis, Robert King, tossed in 49 of the Bombers' points, while teammate H. McCosky added 35 more. Williamsport had a 40-7 halftime lead, but the Bombers' coach apparently had no intention of asking his team to take it easy; the Bombers scored 58 in the second half.

Keep in mind that it was probable that Judyville rarely touched the ball while scoring only 3 second-half points; in those days a center jump was held after every score, and a team with a dominant player could almost always keep control of the ball at its end of the floor.

In February, Judyville's squad headed to Boswell; the Blackhawks actually had seven players on their roster by then, but the visitors took their measure anyway in what must have been a real barnburner, 17-16. At least Judyville had won a real game. In an interesting caveat to the game, I found an "I.H.S.A.A. Eligibility Certification" from Boswell's principal, Edgar Burnette, paper-clipped to the inside cover of the scorebook. It listed the seven eligible Boswell players, including Zerma Trimble and Wilbur Odle.

It is just an old scorebook, but I couldn't help but see in my mind's eye, albeit in grays and blacks and whites, a group of farm boys who just wanted to play ball. I can see them in their "Ralph Jones Professional Basket Ball Shoes," also made by Sears, and I can see them running up and down country roads and gravel highways in Model T's to play in barn lots.

Basketball is different now; it's a faster game with more skilled players who use better equipment. But what the game has become all started for us in places like Judyville.

Overtime
Naming Names, and more…

The Best of the Basketball Stories…

******Author's Note: The six stories in Overtime were left for the last chapter for a reason. Five of them deal with the same topic: old school nicknames. I still receive the occasional letter from readers who find those stories floating around on the Internet.***

The first column in Overtime is the one that gave me my first taste of the front page; it really signaled the end of the line for the regular Sidelines stories…

Growing up in the good old days: It's a wonder we've lived this long February 18, 2004

My older sister tried to kill me when I was 7. She took me to the top of old Mr. Stahl's hill, sat me on her decrepit 20-inch bike in the middle of an oiled gravel road, and gave me a good push. The problem was that she didn't include instructions in her pre-ride pep talk for stopping the bike. She just sent me on my merry way toward the traffic of a busy intersection and a 15-foot drop into the black hole of a concrete culvert.

That quick trip scarred me for life: To this day, I'm still afraid to ride a 20-inch bike down a steep hill... The tale of that near-death experience surfaced as I sat around my in-laws' kitchen table a few nights ago swapping childhood stories with my wife's clan.

It seems as though we all had memories to share about growing up in the good old days, you know, before kids were spoiled by all this stuff we now buy for them.

All of us at the roundtable were "middle-aged"—a term that is only accurate if the average life expectancy is 96 or so—and these trips down Memory Lane seem to take place more often than they used to. They also get one unexpected result: Our kids are discovering just how stupid, and human, their parents once were.

My brother-in-law, Gene Baxter, donated his story about how he and a cousin managed to "coast" their uncle's old Ford Falcon down a long country road without running into a ditch or a tree, not remarkable at all until you realize that he wasn't yet old enough to go to school and his "older" cousin was a second-grader who couldn't even see over the steering wheel.

One of my wife's sisters divulged for the first time in front of her parents that she often climbed out of her upstairs bedroom window and onto the roof late at night to gab with her friends, often precariously close to dropping off into the darkness. It was also interesting that my wife, too, survived backing an uncle's car out of his driveway at a ridiculously young age.

I mentioned how my science-experiment-loving brother once fried eggs in the blistering heat of July on the tin roof of our old shed, then fed them to me, his very young but willing test subject, who often played Igor to his Dr. Frankenstein.

Believe it or not, these stories do have a sports application: Despite rather primitive preventative measures, most kids from my generation survived to tell about their childhoods. A friend recently sent an e-mail to me to that end, and it suggested that despite drinking from vinyl water hoses, not having cell phones, and lacking bike helmets or seat belts, we lived to relate our horror stories years later over the meat trays of holiday get-togethers.

It's true. When I was a kid, not everyone made the basketball team or was guaranteed playing time, and I have to admit that being cut from tryouts hurts quite a bit, but not as badly as that bike crash. Yes, we did play "dodgeball" in gym class—we called it "artillery" then—and like the hungry jaguars we saw on "Mutual of Omaha's Wild Kingdom," we often sought out the weakest of our classmates for annihilation before we, too, fell victim to the biggest and the baddest among us. By the way, many of those who didn't survive dodge ball went on to live productive lives, some fittingly becoming the employers of the goons who pounded them into mush.

In my day (Did I just say that?), very, very few of us had the money to attend a basketball camp; I don't think summer traveling teams existed. You were lucky to just get into a pick-up game at the park, lucky because there was always a line waiting to play. The rule: If you won, you stayed; if you lost, you sat down. No summer coaching, no pump-up tennis shoes, no sports drinks that replenish the electrolytes you've lost. You played, you called your own fouls, and you made your friends and enemies without many adults around to organize the rules for you. We even used to shoot jump shots to determine captains, then allowed them to "choose up" teams. Often, poor players were chosen last or not at all. That smarts a bit, too.

I'm not bashing bottled water, curfews, and bike helmets: My kids have grownup with all three. You see, when I was kid, we did all kinds of things that rules, political correctness, safety measures, and common sense won't allow now. And you know what? For most part, I'd say I was pretty lucky to have just a few scars and some goofy memories to show for it.

Not everything from the good old days was good, and often, if we think about it, not everything that we can now laugh at was very funny. We can make all the fun we want about how kids are overprotected now, how we baby them and give them things we never had. But the world I grew up in was a different world than the one we have now. We may have had the Russians to worry about, but these kids have seen airliners crash into crowded buildings, they anticipate school shootings, and they read about highway snipers on the Internet.

No, we didn't have childproof bottle caps when I was a boy, and most schools held slow learners back a grade or two, but it really is too bad that our kids couldn't have been kids with us.

Police Dogs and Purple Dragons aside, Berries and Brickies live on
December 13, 2000

There's been a good bit of water gone under the bridge since the days when most counties in Indiana had a high school in the middle of every whistlestop and country burg big enough to merit a crossroad or a gas station.

But despite years of consolidation and construction, a few communities in the state have fought to hang onto the tradition of their school nicknames, even as their schools have grown up. Some names have survived the better part of a century, while others have been flushed away by progress or demoted for use at remodeled elementary and middle schools. A few others linger only on nostalgic license plates and sweatshirts and in memory.

A quick check of the 384 high schools belonging to the IHSAA rolls found that the most popular school nickname in the Hoosier State today is Panthers–18 schools use it. Warriors, Tigers, Bulldogs, Eagles, Trojans, Cougars, Knights, Wildcats, and Braves round out the top ten.

Long gone are the days of the Beantowners (Fontanet), Hickories (Colfax), Speedcats (Dunkirk), and Blue Jeans (Monroe City). The Police Dogs hailed from Tippecanoe, the Presidents from South Bend Wilson, and the Purple Dragons hailed from Pinnell. Yet, in tiny Shoals, Logansport, and Hobart, history has won out over progress. The Jug Rox, Berries, and Brickies live on.

Shoals is small—just 254 students in four grades. Tucked away in the center of Martin County, the tiny high school has kept its blue and white, its "On Wisconsin," and its nickname—the Jug Rox—for years. How the school got the name is really no mystery at all. According to Athletic Director Jeff Doyle, about a half-mile west of the White River Bridge on U.S. 50 at Shoals, stands Jug Rock, an "eroded sandstone oddity" that is 20 feet in diameter, and 60 feet high. The rock reminded early pioneers of the earthenware jugs that many of them commonly used. Eventually, the school came, and the name so often associated with the area stuck.

Logansport's nickname, the Berries, is a bit more modern, but its origin more theoretical. In contrast to Shoals, Logansport has nearly 1,100 students. It also plays its basketball in the Berry Bowl, its football in Berry Stadium.

There are two explanations for the nickname. The first comes from an expression used by our grandparents, undoubtedly at a time when raccoon coats and hip flasks were the rage. "They're the berries," was apparently popular in Logansport about 80 years ago. The second theory lies with the loganberry. The town was often, and still is, simply called Logan. Since the old gymnasium in Logansport was shaped like a bowl, it seemed fitting to simply call it the Berry Bowl.

One side note about Logansport that interested me as much as the unique nickname was the story of the school's mascot, as related to me by Kathy Courtad, Athletic Director Greg Fisher's assistant.

In late March 1926, 16 members of the Logansport basketball team were headed to a postseason banquet at the Barnes Hotel. At the entrance, Coach Cliff Wells noticed a small, stuffed cat made of oilcloth. The replica of Felix the Cat was decked out in school colors, so Wells bought it. Curly Hupp, the team captain, eventually stored Felix away in his locker. As a badly needed inspiration for his team the following season, Hupp placed the cat at mid-court in a game in which the Berries eventually staged a winning comeback. Felix went on to survive various surgeries and kidnappings and will celebrate his 75th anniversary with the school at a big party in Logansport in January. The party will be staged along with a Friday night game with rival New Castle.

Hobart was an industrial town in the early 1900s, and the Hobart brickyards employed hundreds of people in northwest Indiana for decades. The brickyards closed down in the depression years of the 1930s, but the nickname stayed in town for the purple and gold-clad school of over 1,100 students.

Hobart's athletic director, Bob Glover, tells me that, "To our knowledge," his school's teams are the only Brickies in the nation, and the mascot and nickname have been copyrighted.

Glover's comments are typical of schools that have maintained their respect for tradition. I've heard it from others, including Ed Gilliland, AD at LaPorte, Hobart's Duneland Conference opponent. How did LaPorte become the Slicers; Switzerland County, the Pacers; and, Rochester, the Zebras? That's fodder for another column in January.

Today, about a quarter of Indiana's high schools share less than a dozen nicknames. I'm sure that games are just as exciting as they once were; there's certainly little doubt that players are more athletic now. But years ago a typical county tournament, for instance, in Montgomery County, could have seen some pretty interesting match-ups.

How about the Wallace Peppers taking on the Waynetown Gladiators, or the Wingate Spartans facing the New Market Purple Flyers? Would you have been interested in watching the Ladoga Canners play the Bowers Blackshirts, or the New Richmond Cardinals tangle with the New Ross Blue Jays?

Indiana basketball truly does have a colorful past.

Looking back in time with the Williamsport Bombers
January 18, 2001

I could almost hear the echoes of fading cheers in the gymnasium in the old Wabash River town of Williamsport last week. It was once the home of the Bombers, and I'm sure had I sat in the north end bleachers atop the subterranean locker rooms, I'd have caught a hint of sweat and tears and smiles of the countless kids who played on that floor long ago.

As promised, I'm returning again to the subject of old school nicknames, a topic that interests me more and more every year.

Many of us can't recall a time when nearly every stop in the road with little more than a barbershop and grain elevator also had a schoolhouse. The nostalgia of those days may have waned a bit, but it is nice to revisit that life every once in a while, even if it's for just a few minutes, as I did in Williamsport.

Although considerably more than a whistlestop in the years just after World War I, LaPorte was searching for a nickname for its school's athletic teams. The result was a city-wide contest. But the story of how LaPorte became the Slicers really began years before. Ed Gilliland, LaPorte's current athletic director, tells me that the nickname's real history got its start in Holland—the one in Europe, not the one in Dubois County —in 1897. It was there that W.A. Van Berkel of Rotterdam conceived the idea of a mechanical meat slicer. By 1909, the first American machines were being manufactured by the U.S. Slicing Machine Company out of Chicago. When the company outgrew its factory six years later, it relocated to LaPorte, and eventually, U.S. Slicing became Berkel Incorporated. It's still there.

The contest followed in the 1920s, and the winning nickname is generally credited to Margaret Elshout, who submitted "Slicers" because her father had migrated to Chicago to work for the company. Apparently, U.S. Slicing had also donated uniforms and supported LaPorte's teams for years, so community goodwill also ran pretty high.

LaPorte's new nickname really didn't catch on until the mid-20s. The school's athletic teams had always been called Orangemen before, and clippings from the old Daily Herald and Argus-Bulletin verify that. But George Allesee Sr. kept promoting the new moniker in his Herald Argus, and it eventually became the standard.

LaPorte has grown to nearly 2,000 students now, but Gilliland proudly notes that, to his knowledge, "the LaPorte Slicers are the only Slicers in the nation."

The story about Rochester's Zebras is less complicated. The Fulton County school of nearly 600 students earned its nickname in 1912. Athletic Director Mark Miller says that his school's basketball team appeared in the state tourney that year in new uniforms that were half black and half white.

The stripes on the new outfits ran vertically, and were designed by the principal and head coach, R.J. Johnson. Fans almost immediately began to identify Rochester's team "as looking like Zebras." As usual, a sportswriter figured into the equation, picking up on the new name and popularizing it through the local newspaper. Miller added that there is a photo of the original Zebras' uniform at the Indiana Basketball Hall of Fame in New Castle, and it can be purchased as a postcard.

A little digging turned up a few other old-time Zebras. Pulaski County's Francesville, now part of West Central High School, and Jonesboro, in Grant County, shared the name with Rochester years ago. Rockport, now part of South Spencer, also wore the black and white. Now, Rochester is the only one remaining.

Another nickname that caught my eye comes from Switzerland County High School, located about as far south and east as you can drive in this state. It's interesting to note that the Switzerland County

Pacers' story grew out of a consolidation in 1966, so theirs is not an old tale at all.

According to John Maxwell, SC's AD, there was a major controversy over where the new school would be built, but the nickname didn't take much thought at all. The popularity of the Indiana Pacers was building in the state by the mid-60s, and the Ohio River Valley Conference Pacers were born.

Switzerland County is located in Vevay, a small Ohio River town. The original plans called for the school to be built upriver near Patriot, another small community, but when the site changed, some enraged parents chose to send their children to Rising Sun, just north in tiny Ohio County. By the way, Rising Sun's nickname is, obviously, the Shiners.

This won't be my last story about nicknames. I can't imagine a time when nearly 800 schools played in our state basketball tournament, but there was, and it was an age when a school's pride was most reflected in its name. There were Green Streaks in Idaville, Gold Bugs in Lincolnville, Scarlets at Beverly, Black Aces in Kingman, and Blue Raiders in Carthage.

On countless Friday nights in mid-winter, it was Oolitic's Bearcats, the Somerset Shamrocks, the Spiceland Stingers, and the Buck Creek Cobras doing battle. On the coldest of those frigid January evenings, it was no doubt quite warm as the Chili Polar Bears, the Winslow Eskimos, or the Eaton Norsemen squared off on the hardwood.

If we listen hard enough, we still might hear them play. I had that chance one night not long ago in an old gym in Williamsport.

Call in the Marines, the Argylls are here
March 13, 2002

Names are not always what they seem. The common Welsh name Bzjxxllwcp is pronounced Jackson. –Mark Twain

I didn't appreciate her then, but my third grade teacher, Mrs. Williamson, had to put up with five Mikes in her class. Despite our angelic desire to learn, she had to endure every one of us simultaneously responding when she asked just one of us something. She eventually gave each of us a nickname, and as long as mine wasn't attached with instructions on how to find the principal's office, I was satisfied.

It seems as though I've been fascinated with names ever since, particularly school nicknames. Even though my grade school name, the Otters, wasn't very fierce, I was still proud of it. I didn't know of any other Otters out there, and I imagined that when we did mix it up with a Warrior or a Red Devil, we'd at least be rabid Otters.

Deep in their collective hearts, I'm certain that over the years every committee, school board, or student council left with the task of giving their new school a nickname, thought they chose the best one, but it's obvious that the golden age of nicknaming in Indiana had to have been in the 20s and 30s.

The fact is that about a fourth of Indiana's high schools share about a dozen nicknames. Those quaint and original homegrown names are passing away, and even more alarming, so are the people who know the origins of those names. After a quick glance at the IHSAA

Handbook, I contacted a few athletic directors, hopeful that they might be able to tell me the story behind their school's nickname. A few shared what they knew.

For instance, I've always been interested as to why Andrean High School in Merrillville carried the nickname, "The Fighting 59ers." AD Bill Mueller's matter-of-fact response set me straight. Andrean was built in 1959, he told me. The school's address is 5959 Broadway in Merrillville, too. That's it: end of story.

I wrote little Hamilton High School in Hamilton intrigued with why they are the Marines. Athletic Director Brian Miller was proud of the fact that his Marines are one of only two in the country, the other being on Long Island.

"According to our former principal, Gus Haughey, we got our nickname in 1938," Miller said. "The school was then located on the shore of Hamilton Lake and several marinas were there. The U.S. Marines were also in the news a lot in those days with their forays into places like Nicaragua. So, putting those two facts together is how we came up with our nickname, Marines," Miller added.

By far the longest of the responses I got was from yet another small school, Madison-Grant, near Fairmount, the home of an average high school guard who made a name for himself in other endeavors: James Dean. First-year athletic director Joe Toth gave me a full rundown on the Madison-Grant Argylls. That's Argylls, not Argyles, as in socks, although the terms are related. I have to admit, I had images of Scottish plaid warm-ups, bagpipes in the school band, even warm haggis—trust me, never order this off the menu—sold at the concession stand. Toth wasn't exactly sure why Madison-Grant took the name, but he was certain that, "We are the only school in the United States with the nickname Argylls."

One thing is obvious: whoever selected this school nickname put some thought into it. "Argylls history has a long and proud Scottish tradition dating back to 1685," Toth says. "The word Argyll means 'home' and 'Our own people,' and comes from Argyllshire, a community in Scotland. The people known as Argylls were Scottish warriors and statesmen back in the 17th and 18th centuries," Toth mentioned.

By the way, Madison-Grant also has a boar's head on its school crest, primarily because one of the early dukes of the Campbell clan—who fought under the name of the Argylls—was killed fighting a wild boar that had been terrorizing his community. I'd venture to guess that Madison-Grant is the only school in the country with a boar on its crest too. There may be a number of Panthers and Tigers and Bulldogs in Indiana, but only one Argyll boar.

I won't lie to you; I still like the old names: the ones that passed by when their schools were passed up. The Bedford Stonecutters, the Sugar Creek Crickets, and the Warren Lightning Five may be no more, but there are still quite a few schools that still have the spirit. For instance, there's the Wolfpack in Crawford County, the Bombers in Rensselaer, and the Oilers in Whiting.

Unique nicknames aren't native to Indiana alone. It may be apocryphal, but I heard there's a school in Missouri whose nickname is the Kewpies. Seems a player back in the 20s picked himself up from the floor looking like a Kewpie Doll, and the name was born.

And I thought it was tough being a mean Otter.

It doesn't take much for me to name names
January 25, 2006

It's no secret that I enjoy talking about old high school nicknames; I've done several columns on the subject before. I usually wait a little while before I write about a topic for a second (or third) time, but when Fred Myers of Riley dropped a letter to me a few weeks ago pointing out a potential mistake I made about a nickname, I just couldn't resist going into it again. After all, it has been a couple of years.

Most of the letters I get are positive, and Fred's was no exception; he simply reminded me, politely, that I needed to double-check my facts about the high school nickname for Quincy, a tiny burg in the uppermost northeast corner of Owen County. In my yearly pre-tournament quiz for the Pizza Hut Wabash Valley Classic, I had said that Quincy's team was the Aces and that the school had consolidated into Owen Valley.

Fred suggested that the Aces hailed from Freedom, another small town just down Indiana 67 to the southwest, and he was right; the Aces did come from Freedom. But after doing a little research, I discovered that the nickname also belonged to Quincy. That fact should have made me happy, but along with the confirmation that I was right about the name, I also found out that Quincy eventually consolidated across county lines into Cloverdale High School, not into Owen Valley. So on that point, I was wrong, and Fred's letter taught me something after all.

There's something fascinating about the pre-consolidated high school era in Indiana and the unique nicknames from those old days. I don't have anything against the new—but rather generic—names of the latest generation of schools, but not everything that's newer is necessarily better.

From Acton to Algiers, Lagro to Losantville, and Saluda to Selvin, it seems as though just about every small Indiana community had a school, a nickname, and a unique story, all its own. Some of the names weren't the most politically correct, but they are an enjoyable trip to the past.

My favorite names are either melodious or ominous or a little bit of both. It must have been pretty intimidating to know you had to square off on a Friday night in the dead of winter against the Buck Creek Cobras, the Holton Warhorses, the Kennard Leopardcats, or the Swayzee Speedkings. I don't know if I'd have enjoyed facing the Tippecanoe Police Dogs, the Waynetown Gladiators, the Banquo Ghosts, or the Redkey Wolves on the road either.

Want to play against a bunch of Gorillas? That's exactly what you'd have had to do had you walked into the gym at Hartford City for a game. You could have expected to have seen Haymakers thrown around had you played in Hayden, and at Summitville you'd have tipped off against the Goblins.

Quick, say Pinnell Purple Dragons three times before you move on...

I think there's a good bit of history we can learn from the old names; many of the folks in the proud little towns in the old days chose nicknames and mascots that either echoed their town's name or some bit of history associated with it. That was obviously the case for the Bedford Stonecutters, the Edwardsport Powers, the Maukport Pilots, the Klondike Nuggets, the Ladoga Canners (there was a canning factory in town), the Marengo Cavemen, the Monon Railroaders, the Remington Rifles, and the South Bend Wilson Presidents. That was surely true of the Boston Terriers, the Buffalo Bison, the Lincoln Railsplitters, and the Stinesville Quarry Lads too.

Some schools simply used the town's name as part of its school nickname. The Beaver Dam Beavers, the Clarks Hill Hillers, the Huntingburg Happy Hunters, the Kingsbury Kings, the Lyons Lions, the Midland Middies, and the Mulberry Berries, for instance. The Oil Township Oilers, Otter Creek Otters, Oaktown Oaks, Poseyville Posies, and Rome City Romans did too. It was pretty obvious that the Sir Walters came from Raleigh and the Pine Knots from Pine Village.

It seems to me that color was often considered more important in days gone by too. There was a virtual rainbow on display when the Alquina Blue Arrows or the Arlington Purple Breezes played. Just think of the crayon box of beauty when the Carthage Blue Raiders, the Clear Spring Purple Warriors, the Etna Green Cubs, the Lincolnville Gold Bugs, or the Medaryville Black Horses ran onto the floor. New Market had their Purple Flyers, New Waverly had the Scarlets, and, of course, Terre Haute was home to Purple Eagles, Black Cats, Red Streaks, and Golden Bears.

You would think that some nicknames were so unique that only one school could have had it, but that's not the case. There was only one Raccoons (Bridgeton) and one Blackshirts (Bowers), only one Windmills

(Butler) too, and there surely could have only been one Wampus Cats (Cambridge City), while the Kangaroos called only Kirkland home. But there were at least two schools that shared Tornadoes (Gary Emerson and Griffin), while Mecca had its Arabs and Markleville its Arabians. Ridgeville, Riley, and Russiaville were the Cossacks; Plainville, Perry Central, and Wanatah had the Midgets; and Yankeetown and Young America shared the Yanks. I always knew that Pimento and Wallace were both home to the Peppers.

I'm not sure if they ever played on their own floor, but Spartanburg was home to the Tomcats. Now, there's a team ready for the road if I ever heard of one. Did they look forward to running into the Orioles (Lima), the Bluebirds (Ninevah), or the Wrens (Patoka)?

From Coal City (the Colts) to Deer Creek (the Crickets), from Kirklan (the Travelers) to Milton (the Sharpshooters), Indiana sought progress through consolidation, and left much of its history to be remembered only on nostalgic coffee mugs, license plates, and garage sale yearbooks.

Illinois has its share of unique nicknames too
February 28, 2007

Over the years, I've written at least four columns about unique school nicknames, but Casey resident Jim Blome reminded me in a letter about a year ago that I've never done a story about interesting names from Illinois schools. I think it's time I remedied that error.

Along with his letter, Jim sent a rather long list of names I might want to include in my story, a virtual nickname bonanza that I would normally have had to labor to put together myself through research. He gave credit for the list to long-time Marshall Lions basketball coach, Nellie Bennett, so I want to be sure to pass my thanks on to him, as well.

Along the way, I also ran into yet another source for my material, Fred Willman's "Why Mascots Have Tales" (IHSA, 2005, $20.00). Willman, a retired teacher, told me via e-mail that he got interested in school nicknames because, "I like sports, and I like good stories."

The Naperville native's book appears to be filled with both. According to Willman, there are 788 high schools in Illinois; they share 250 nicknames, 144 of which he deemed "unusual."

For most part, school nicknames from years ago often reflected their communities. In Indiana, as across the country, local businesses (Ladoga Canners), ethnic groups (Mecca Arabs), and tales from history (Vincennes Alices) were often the genesis for the local school's moniker. Likewise, in Illinois, there is DeKalb (the Barbs were named for the barbed wire manufactured there), Addison Driscoll (the Highlanders), and Lincoln (the Railsplitters). Nicknames were a matter of pride, perhaps even prejudices, but at least they were unique. Illinois, like Indiana, has lost many of those names to consolidation, a few more to political correctness.

When I glanced down Bennett's list—and I want to make it clear that, to my knowledge, all of these schools still exist—I was first attracted to colorful nicknames. The Alexis Red Storm caught my eye, as did the Aledo Green Dragons, the Carthage Blue Boys, the Galesburg Silver Streaks, the Mattoon Green Wave, the

Jacksonville Crimsons, the Knoxville Blue Bullets, the Litchfield Purple Panthers, and the Mt. Carmel Golden Aces. Andy Amey's personal favorite—the Arcola Purple Riders—made the list too.

The absolute coolest name to me was the Illinois Valley Grey Ghosts; there is nothing generic about being a Grey Ghost.

In light of the protest over the retirement of Chief Illiniwek at the University of Illinois, a number of high schools surely have had to take a look at their nicknames over the years too, and Antioch High School is one of them. According to Willman, Antioch, the home of the Sequoits, is actually using a word that is Native American in origin, but only by a long stretch. There is no tribe of that name, only an Iroquois word, "Sadaquoit," a term given to a stream that runs in upper-state New York in Oneida County. When settlers moved from there to Illinois, they used a variance of the word. By the way, the Aurora West Blackhawks, Cahokia Comanches, and Mooseheart Mohawks use names of Native American tribes. Pittsfield, a central Illinois town where Abraham Lincoln once roamed, is known as the "Hog Capital of the Midwest," but students in its school with an enrollment of about 480 still call themselves Saukees, presumably after the Sauk Indians.

There was certainly an adventuring spirit at work when many Illinois schools chose nicknames. The Belleville Aithoff Crusaders and Alton Marquette Explorers were among that group, as were the Argo Argonauts, the Chicago Mt. Carmel Caravan, and the Mudelein Corsairs. The military was represented as well with schools like the Argenta-Oreana Bombers, the Bunker Hill Minutemen, the Ullin Centurians, the Chicago

Marshall Commandoes, the Farragut Admirals, the Decatur MacArthur Generals, the Milledgeville Missiles, and the Stream-wood Sabres.

If history is your subject of choice, make the connection between Monticello and its Sages, Arthur and its Knights, East St. Louis and its Fliers, Fulton and its Steamers, Polo and its Marcos, and Springfield and its Senators. You can find Turks in Tremont, Saxons in Schaumburg, Norsemen in Newark, and Pharoahs in Tamms. If meteorology interests you, hang on to your hat in Catlin Salt Fork (Hurricanes), Taylorville (Tornadoes), and LaHarpe (Cyclones). You can watch the Meteors in Marissa and keep your eye on the North Stars at St. Charles North.

I know that Illinois is a civilized place, but it still has its Dragons (Divernon), Demons (Dongola), and Vandals (Vandalia), and, as most towns do, its Tomcats (Aurora East). It is a state abundant in wildlife, substantiated by the Kewanee Weathersfield Flying Geese, Indian Creek's Timberwolves, Colfax's Mustangs, Fisher's Bunnies (Does Fighin' Bunnies sound better?), Havana's Ducks, McLeansboro's Foxes, Mounds Meridian's Bobcats, and Petersburg Porta's Blue Jays. The Scotties from Waverly, Terriers from Carbondale, and Greyhounds from Chicago Hubbard at least sound more domesticated.

Willman's "unusual" category must be full too. There's Appleknockers in Cobden, Orphans in Centralia (the girls' teams are the Orphan Annies), Flaming Hearts in Effingham, WhipPurs in Hampshire, Cornjerkers in Hoopeston, Caxys in Lake Forest, and, of course, Wooden Shoes in Teutopolis (their junior high teams are reportedly called Booties).

By the way, have you ever heard about some of the unusual school nicknames in Kentucky? Well, there's the Somerset Briar Jumpers and the Lloyd Memorial Juggernauts and the. . .

The Best of the Basketball Stories...

Photographs

The Coach: Bernard Gideon (far left) stands with his 1957-58 Montezuma Aztecs squad. Bernard is the topic of both ***Coach cherishes memories but also likes changes*** on page 6 and ***No one can really fill the vacant chair*** on page 84.

Courtesy of Larry Bartlow

The Best: Indiana State's Larry Bird makes his move at a packed Hulman Center in 1979. Memories of watching Bird play came to the author on the eve of the retirement of his and Duane Kleuh's jerseys in ***What I remember about Larry Bird*** on page 136.

Courtesy of Mark Bennett and the Terre Haute Tribune-Star

Seize the Day: Howard Mathas (3) poses with his 1936 Montezuma Aztecs. Howard went on to coach at a number of Wabash Valley high schools, including Wiley's Red Streaks. His story is told in ***It's time to seize the day, boys*** on page 169.

Courtesy of the Montezuma Alumni Association

A Lion That Was Once a Tiger: Marshall Lions supporter Murray Melton (third from the left on the front row) was once a fine player for the 1942-43 Hutsonville Tigers. See ***Murray Melton, a real All-American*** on page 91.

Courtesy of Bill Melton

Teammates to the End: Glenn Coach Jack Williams holds the ball surrounded by his 1950-51 Pirates' starting five of (left to right) Cliff Phillips, Oscar Session, Charlie Session, Dick Richmond, and Mike Dragon. Glenn won 30 consecutive games before losing in the semi-state tournament to Evansville Reitz. A dispute over Charlie's age led to the team eventually being stripped of its victories; the team won back-to-back Wabash Valley Tournament championships. The Pirates and Williams are the basis of ***Teammates to the very end*** on page 154.

Courtesy of Kadel's Photography and Fred Foxworthy

Wildcat: Clinton's Mike Carty (white) avoids a trapping Covington defense in a 1969 game on the Wildcats' floor. Carty's memories are featured in ***Cold weather just another excuse to talk basketball*** on page 95.

Courtesy of The Old Gold and Black

Towels Please: Craig McKee (left) and Paul Johnson (right) as they appeared during their tenures as basketball managers at Terre Haute North and Riverton Parke High Schools. McKee, shown in 1975, was nicknamed "The Professor"; Johnson, shown in 1992, was affectionately called "PJ." Both men's careers as managers are told in ***Duties of manager helped in preparation for life*** on page 65.

Courtesy of Craig McKee and Joanie Lunsford

Neighbors: The 1932 Rosedale squad won the Parke County Tournament; several from this team played in the championship game of the Wabash Valley Tournament in 1934. Neighbors Herman Huxford and Everett Newton (first and second from the left in the back row) played on the team. .

Courtesy of Everett Newton

Superman: The author's cousin, Roger Herzog (44), shown in high school action in 1968, is the subject for ***Watching Superman play basketball*** on page 113.
Courtesy of Rosedale Alumni Assoc.

Little Man; Big Heart: Mickey Kor is shown in typical Purdue University apparel and with students he's taught about the Holocaust. See ***The best little big man who never played*** on page 116. **Courtesy of Fort Branch Community School**

Happy to Play: Joyce Spencer (left) and Kristin Colletti loved to be on the floor. Joyce's story is told in ***Photograph recalls flood of memories*** on page 32, and Kristin's follows in ***There's plenty in sports world to feel warm and fuzzy about*** on page 41. **Courtesy of The Parke County Sentinel and Tim Terry**

A Jewel: Longtime coach and administrator Hubert McHargue (far left) is shown with his 1942-43 Rosedale Hotshots after they'd won the Parke County Tournament at Bellmore and qualified for the final 16-team field of the Wabash Valley Tournament in Terre Haute. The author spoke with McHargue as he neared age 90 and shared the old coach's views in ***McHargue, a diamond in my backyard*** on page 101. **Courtesy of the Rosedale Alumni Association**

Dream Coats: The author, with buddies, Joe Huxford (left) and Sam Ball (right) wears the jacket that inspired ***Joseph's amazing Technicolor dream coats*** on page 160. **Photo by Joanie Lunsford**

Basketball Glory: Pizza Hut Wabash Valley Classic founder Gary Fears (center of back row) holds the trophy with his Honey Creek teammates after winning a Wabash Valley Prelim game against Decker Chapel in 1960. Over the years, more than a dozen ***Sidelines*** columns have been devoted to the Classic and its great atmosphere.

Courtesy of Gary Fears

Meeting Oscar: Don Layton (left, dark uniform) tangles with Oscar Robertson in a game between Layton's Indianapolis Howe team and Crispus Attucks in 1954. Layton was considered one of the best athletes in Marion County and went on to a long teaching career in the Department of History at Indiana State University. His story is featured in ***A professor at the top of his game*** on page 108.

Courtesy of the Indianapolis Star and Don Layton

What We've Lost: The 1922 Rosedale Hotshots with Coach Clyde Cunningham (back right) as they appeared about the time they played the likes of Concannon and Fontanet. This photo appeared in the school's annual, *The Outlook*, the subject of ***It's not how much we've gained, but how much we've lost*** on page 176.
Courtesy of Judy Hughes

The Disch: Garfield's Terry Dischinger makes a move for Purdue. Dischinger was one of three Olympic Gold medalists featured in ***Winners in every sense of the word*** on page 179.
Courtesy of Mike McCormick

Hoops Heaven: The author's son, Evan, stands under a side goal in the old gymnasium in Knightstown, Indiana. The writer's visit to Knightstown in 1998 is the topic of ***Author finds hoops heaven in Hickory*** on page 30.

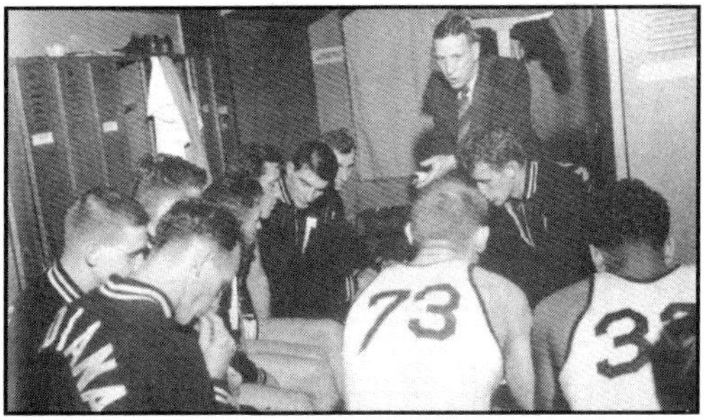

The Wizard of Terre Haute: John Wooden spent two seasons at Indiana State University before heading to UCLA; here, he instructs his team at halftime of a game in 1947. Wooden is the subject of ***Despite age, Wooden remains refreshingly new*** on page 61.

Courtesy of Mike McCormick

A Wildcat, a Pepper, and Two Aztecs: Bud "Buddy" McCammon (left), Larry Adamson (middle) and Annie Branson and Lisa Persinger (right) all proudly wore the team colors of Clinton, Pimento, and Montezuma.

McCammon works on his shot prior to a game in the 1949-1950 season; his story inspired ***Times change for Clinton man, but not memories*** on page 50. Adamson was a guard for the Peppers and is shown in 1960; his memories were included in ***Cold weather just another excuse to talk basketball*** on page 95. Branson and Persinger are shown as junior-varsity players for the 1983 Lady Aztecs; their story is told in ***Another year gone, but good memories keep coming back*** on page 99.

Photos courtesy of Martha McCammon, Larry Adamson, and Impressions

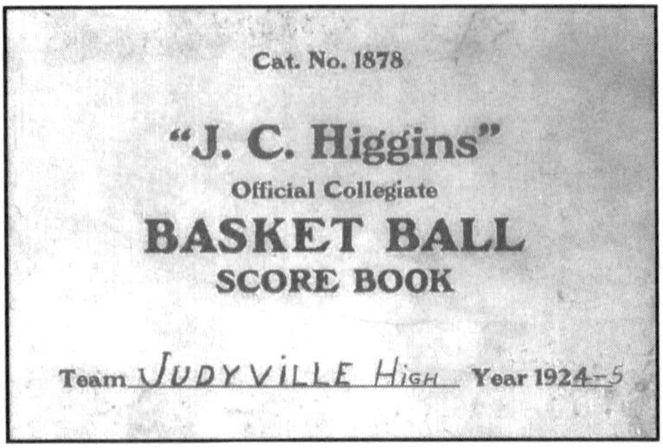

History Book: The basketball scorebook for tiny Judyville High School provided writing fodder for ***Thumbing through a real history book*** on page 183. Judyville, located in Warren County, like so many Indiana schools of its era, couldn't survive consolidation.

Poetry in Motion: Olympic long jump Gold Medalist and Garfield High School grad, Greg Bell (right) recited his poem, "I Believe In You," at a ceremony honoring him, Clyde Lovellette, and Terry Dischinger in 2007. Bell, along with the others, is featured in ***Winners in every sense of the word*** on page 179.
Courtesy of Mike McCormick

Whistle Blower: Veteran official Steve Morris shows his love for the game every time he walks onto the floor in his referee's jersey. Steve's devotion to his craft is the topic of ***Basketball officials may have the greatest love of the game*** on page 71. **Courtesy of Steve Morris**

Meeting Her Hero: Stacey Greene (above) with former Purdue Coach Gene Keady was at one time the most faithful of Keady and Purdue fans but now works in the football office at Indiana State University. Football was far from Stacey's mind in 1997 when she was featured in ***Nothing can keep this Purdue fan far from the court*** on page 17. **Courtesy of Stacey Greene**